"Part inspiration, part practical guide, Jeeyoon Kim serves up nuggets of wisdom—whether you're truly stuck or just seeking a nudge. Open up to any page the next time you need a pep talk."

—**Karen Zorn**, President of Longy School of Music

"In the rarified world of classical music, talent is never enough. With *Whenever You're Ready*, classical pianist Jeeyoon Kim reveals the secrets of success in five life-changing movements. Charming, insightful, inspiring, and practical, this is a must-read for anyone with dreams."

—**Tim Wilson**, Executive Director of Western Arts Alliance

"I wish I had had this book at the beginning of my musical career, and I am fortunate to have it now. Jeeyoon has given us an inspirational set of tools at our fingertips. I would recommend this book to any aspiring performer and established professional."

—**John Stubbs**, Conductor and Music Director of
California Ballet Company

"What a gem! This book is a gracious invitation to fully engage with what it means to compose our life in an intentional and thoughtful way. As accessible and eloquent as Jeeyoon's presence on stage, the pages are full of practical wisdom that inspire the reader to deeper reflection on their own performance. Each chapter closes with a gentle summons to try something new and in doing so, emerge fully onto the stage of our life when we are ready."

—**Julianne Miranda**, ACC, Certified Life Coach
and Bereavement Specialist

"*Whenever You're Ready* is the perfect resource guide for anyone who wants to improve upon their long-term professional or personal goals. It weaves together practical, easy-to-follow principles for success, recommendations to improve personal habits, and suggestions to find that ever-so-difficult balance within. For musicians and non-musicians alike, Jeeyoon's well-thought-out musical structure and beautifully crafted narrative give you the lift you need to improve your mindset and perhaps appreciate some beautiful music in the process."

—**Tommy Phillips**, President and Artistic Director of the Philharmonic Society of Orange County

"Jeeyoon combines her contagious passion for music and joy for life into a thought-provoking guidebook for a more productive and satisfying existence. Pianos are welcome, but definitely not required."

—**Pedja Muzijevic**, pianist, artistic administrator at Baryshnikov Arts Center, and artistic advisor to Tippet Rise Art Center

"Jeeyoon's brilliant artistry is only matched by her unique ability to reach the audience, manage her own career, and constantly reinvent herself as a true artist in the 21st century."

—**Jim Fung**, Founder of Captivate Artists, presenter, and promoter

"What this book reveals is a very courageous lady who chose not to follow but to create her own path. And in so doing Jeeyoon became an inspiration for thousands who have a dream. She made that first impossible step and set an example for others to follow. The book is the triumph of a dream realized."

—**Allen T. Brown**, author of *Dancing Through Life*

"Jeeyoon Kim is an extraordinarily talented pianist whose musicianship combines brilliant technical skills, deeply personal expressivity, and a communicative approach to concertizing that has captured the hearts and minds of audiences wherever she performs. In *Whenever You're Ready*, Ms. Kim offers a practical guide to creating a successful career. Distilled from principles that she formulated while developing her own career, she presents a step-by-step methodology for achieving a lifestyle directed to succeed in any walk of life. The combination of life-enriching daily routines, both physical and mental, and supplemental exercises are designed to create an orderly life that should enrich anyone's personal as well as artistic goals. Written with a deep, abiding love of music, this book avoids intellectualizing while providing a user-friendly way of developing routines that, if diligently applied, can enhance career goals as well as structure the fulfillment of other life goals."

—**Lewis M. Smoley**, president of Classical Podcasts

"Inspiring yet practical! Jeeyoon provides a tool kit that demystifies the creativity within us and welcomes us to keep trying to find our own path in life."

—**Eunbi Kim**, pianist and co-founder of bespoken

"What enlightening and delightful storytelling by an award-winning performing artist! Jeeyoon finally reveals secrets to her life success as a pianist and educator. Reading her book was a truly life-changing, magical experience, just like attending one of her breathtaking piano concerts for the first time."

—**Kyunghee Clara Hayashigawa**, educator and pianist

"A captivating journey into the heart and soul of a concert pianist. She also has the heart of a teacher and presents to the reader, based on personal experience, highly effective tools to succeed in real-life circumstances, both personally and professionally, and does so with candor, kindness, and thoughtfulness. I highly recommend this wonderfully written book to my family, friends, colleagues, and students."

—**John Corban,** Independent piano teacher based in Oregon

"What a pleasure to read. It feels like sitting at a coffee shop with Jeeyoon and discussing life and music for hours. Jeeyoon effortlessly convinces and motivates us to use good habits and hard work to achieve amazing results. She shows us not only what is possible, but how to have endless fun on the way."

—**Igor Pandurski,** violinist from San Diego Symphony

WHENEVER
YOU'RE

Jeeyoon Kim

WHENEVER YOU'RE

Ready

How to Compose the Life of Your Dreams

GREENLEAF
BOOK GROUP PRESS

Published by Greenleaf Book Group Press
Austin, Texas
www.gbgpress.com

Distributed by Greenleaf Book Group

For ordering information or special discounts for bulk purchases, please contact Greenleaf Book Group at PO Box 91869, Austin, TX 78709, 512.891.6100.

Design and composition by Greenleaf Book Group
Cover design by Greenleaf Book Group

Publisher's Cataloging-in-Publication data is available.

Print ISBN: 978-1-62634-856-1

eBook ISBN: 978-1-62634-857-8

Part of the Tree Neutral® program, which offsets the number of trees consumed in the production and printing of this book by taking proactive steps, such as planting trees in direct proportion to the number of trees used: www.treeneutral.com

TreeNeutral

Printed in the United States of America on acid-free paper

21 22 23 24 25 26   10 9 8 7 6 5 4 3 2 1

First Edition

Dedicated to Allen T. Brown

CONTENTS

PRELUDE

*J*t is about thirty minutes before the concert begins, and I am standing in the greenroom in Carnegie Hall. The notion of time seems to be distorted at this moment, as if the weight of a tick on a clock is much slower and heavier in this room. I have imagined this moment millions of times in my head, and now that it's a reality, I am not quite sure exactly what I am feeling.

In some ways, it feels like a dream. *Am I dreaming?* I pinch myself. *Of course not.* I am fully awake. When I look at myself in the mirror, it's as if I am looking at someone I don't know. Then I start to talk to myself. "You are loved. You are loving. People in the audience are there to receive what music gives them. You are excited, and they are excited. The space is full of love, and you don't have to do anything more than just become a vessel for the music. The music will speak for itself. You are grateful for this very moment. Now, Jeeyoon, go out to the stage, smile, and play as if this is your last concert and your last day. You have only this moment. Live it fully. You are more than enough."

During most of my time in the greenroom, I am doing breathing exercises and repeating those sentences to myself. Then, after reciting a quick "thank you" prayer to God, I give my reflection in the mirror a big smile and walk toward the stage door.

One minute before 7:30 p.m., I hear the chatting noises from the audience fading into the background.

A stage manager who looks to be about sixty-five smiles at me and says gently, "Whenever you're ready."

But am I ready? I feel the usual butterflies in my stomach, a familiar sensation in my body every time before a concert.

Without making any judgment of whether this is good or bad, I close my eyes and focus on the excitement and courage coming from somewhere deep within me. As the stage guy holds the door open, I look at him and nod.

Then, there it is: the beautiful stage with shining chandeliers and the cheerful clapping of the audience. The magic of music is about to begin.

THE TOOLS IN THIS BOOK

As a pianist, I am often asked what it is like to be on a stage like Carnegie Hall, what it is like to be a pianist on any stage, or behind the stage in my daily life. Many people think I have a special "talent," as if I were born with the skill for what I do. To be honest, I wish I had a magic potion I could whip out every time I give a concert, so that I could play any piece I like without thousands of hours of practice, and could perform without feeling jittery nerves in public. But there is no such potion, and the reality is quite the opposite. Being onstage never does get easier over time, and performing always feels raw and new, requiring my whole being to be exposed and vulnerable all over again.

As a teacher, I strongly believe that we make progress over time, with a deliberate practice. Because of my own personal trials and errors for the past twenty years of performing, practicing, and teaching, one thing has become much more clear now: Being a pianist never gets easier, but it is beautiful that way. There's no need to sugarcoat it or, conversely, become frustrated, as it will always be difficult; rather, learn to dance with the storm, believing that the storm is strengthening our souls.

In this book, I will share all of the tools that I employ behind the scenes to deal with my career as a pianist. I realized what I've discovered over the years is not only useful for a concert pianist, but also for life in general. Being a musician has helped me shape my life, and I've come to see that these tools are valuable to everyone. If I can do it, you can do it too.

MOVEMENTS

I constructed this book as if it is a concert for you. A composer often separates their entire work into various *movements*. For example, a sonata by Chopin in B minor has four movements, and each movement has its own structure and feeling to express. I have five movements in this concert for you, each one with a different purpose.

The first movement is about the actual work of a pianist, how I form habits and apply a concept of persistence in my daily practice life. The second movement is about the mind, about how important it is to guide our minds in positive ways in order to have a happy life. The third movement is about waking up our creative inner child, and the importance of dreaming, creating, and having fun. In the fourth movement, I talk about making connections and discuss in depth how a healthy relationship with ourselves and others strengthens our life journey. In the fifth and final movement, I talk about the body. I find that the daily actions and rituals that consist of caring for my body and my surroundings have a significant effect on me as a person and a pianist, so I could not skip such an important concept in this concert for you.

INTERMISSIONS

Then there will be four intermissions in between each movement. Just like when you go to a concert, an intermission provides a time to refresh yourself physically and mentally for the next course of musical experience. I imagined the same effect for you to have this short intermission piece between the movements. Except this time, the intermission is now about a piece of music itself. I've selected four different pieces of music that are close to my heart and talk briefly in the way I would talk in my master classes or onstage for an audience. I hope you take your time in these intermissions to refresh yourself before you resume the next movement.

YOUR OWN PERFORMANCE

At the end of each chapter, there are activities for you to apply in your own life. This is where you get to practice your tunes for your performance in your life. I hope you take your time to practice each concept in a tangible way and do your best to make them work for you.

Of course, I made sure to have an encore in this concert at the end as well. I wouldn't want to leave this concert stage without playing one final piece for us to share.

In the September–October 2014 *Swimmer Magazine*, they featured me as a cover model and wrote an interesting article about how I use swimming as cross-training for being a concert pianist. They discussed how I prepare myself mentally, physically, and emotionally to be on a stage in water, swimming back and forth in a pool lane. For me, swimming shares many of the same features as practicing the piano; I listen to my inner voice in my head while I move my body and feel the emotion. Both are solitary journeys.

In fact, that is where I got the idea for writing this book. Whether we have piano keys before us or not, we all have a stage, called life. This is a book for whoever wants to be more equipped on the stage of life, developing tools to be more of the person you were meant to be and perhaps gaining just that little bit more courage and strength within yourself to walk toward the crowds when it is time to perform. I would walk with you in spirit as you go through your life, giving that sense of hope. This book has its place between you and the stage door of your life, with tools that may help your performance . . .

"*Whenever you're ready.*"

MOVEMENT #1

Practice until Practicing Is a Part of Your Normal Life

1

HABITS WIN OUT OVER WILLPOWER

*I*n 1984, in an area called Gaegum, in the city of Busan, South Korea, I vividly remember the path I took to get to a small piano institute. There was a tiny grocery store where the shopkeeper always sat outside and waved at me, saying, "Have a great day, Little Pie." Passing him, I came to a street food vendor who sold rice cakes with red-pepper paste that were called *duk bok gi*. I was always tempted to have one or two on my way to the institute, which would cost me about a quarter. But at four years old, I felt that I shouldn't use up all the coins in my pocket, so I only ate them once in a while. For a little girl like myself, the path to the institute seemed to be at least a mile long, though it was probably only two blocks from my house.

I walked to the institute every day except Saturday and Sunday, and I always walked alone. Because both of my parents were busy running the children's clothing business they owned, keeping up with my daily routine was my own responsibility, and I remember taking it very seriously. No one had to tell me when to go to the institute. Every afternoon at about two o'clock, I grabbed my piano bag and went to the door.

On the exterior, the piano institute was like a residential home, but inside there were many small rooms, and in each room was a piano. The floors were wooden, and we took our shoes off as we entered the room. Each day, when I arrived at the institute, my piano instructor always greeted me with a warm smile.

> It is about creating a habit so you don't have to think about *when* you will do the task.

Even though she might have been in the middle of another lesson, she made sure to talk to me and made sure I knew which piano room I should go into. Once I sat down at a piano, I started with a finger exercise called "Hanon."[1] My teacher had previously drawn ten to twenty apples inside my piano book, which I drew a line through as I completed each repetition.

It wasn't until later that I realized all of these lessons were helping me build an important habit that would last my lifetime. Walking to a piano institute every day when I was four years old was something I did, like brushing my teeth or eating breakfast. I went there, I sat down, and I played piano. The social aspect of the whole scene, including meeting my friends from the institute along the way and seeing my piano teacher every day, was something I also looked forward to.

People tell me that I must have a strong will for practicing piano, as if I have something different than they have. But the truth is, I've never considered myself as having more drive or motivation than anyone else. I just had a system in place that made it easy for me to keep doing it.

I have discovered that it is much easier to do something if I do it

---

1   Hanon was a French pedagogue who was famous for his method of developing finger exercises. I don't use them anymore in my own playing, nor do I use them in my teaching. It's a tedious and rather boring approach, though it was used widely in piano education in the 1980s.

regularly rather than sporadically. If I practice piano only three times a week, then it is actually harder for me to keep practicing than if I practice every day. Even now, some thirty-five years later and without fail, my first task in the morning after breakfast is to sit down at the piano and start my first practice session. It is not my will that makes me sit down at the piano, but my lifelong habit, which has helped me push forward.

> The truth is that doing something consistently is easier than doing it sporadically.

I had a student who recently told me about how difficult it was to maintain a steady practice schedule and asked for my advice. I asked him when he practiced the piano, and he said, "Whenever I have time in a day." His practice time varied, depending on the day. If he had a thirty-minute block of time at some point, he practiced. However, those blocks of time easily faded away with other tasks during the day. By the time he came back to me for a lesson, he had maybe managed to find two or three blocks of time each week to practice, even though he planned and hoped to practice daily.

I told him to try building a new practice habit around one habit that he already had each day. He said he already had a habit of brewing an afternoon coffee each day after work, so I asked if he could combine an afternoon coffee with practicing piano for ten minutes. I knew he could play longer than that, but in order to build a habit, he needed to start small. I asked him to practice piano for twenty-one consecutive days, but for only ten minutes each day with his afternoon coffee; if he wanted to do more practice later or earlier at some point in the day, he was welcome to add more. But in that afternoon-coffee practice session, he was asked to practice only ten minutes. At first, he said he was tempted to do more than that bare minimum, but I advised him to keep it light and manageable to be consistent.

Otherwise, he might start one day with thirty or forty minutes of practice with an afternoon coffee, then the next day or so, he may end up thinking he had other tasks he needed to do and being unable to build the routine into a habit.

The results were quite impressive. After twenty-one days of practicing for ten minutes after coffee, he was now allowed to add more time to his afternoon practice session. He was somewhat relieved that he could now practice longer in his newly established routine. Before he knew it, he always associated his afternoon coffee with piano practice. And over time, his daily habit helped him become a better pianist.

Back in my youth, when I walked every afternoon to that piano institute, I spent the first fifteen to twenty minutes practicing by myself, followed by ten minutes of lessons with my teacher. I always left there feeling that it was so much fun. I was never overwhelmed or exhausted. I never thought about *when* I would go to the piano institute, as it was always at the exact same time of day: around two o'clock in the afternoon.

> It is not willpower but a *habit* that helps you get to where you want to be.

To this day, I maintain a consistent habit, though now I practice in the mornings. By about nine, as soon as I finish breakfast, I am on my piano bench—one activity flows naturally into the next, like clockwork. If I had to think of *when* I would practice every time I woke up, I don't think I could keep up with my good practice routine, as I would be spending lots of mental energy thinking of the "when" rather than the work itself. The goal for me is to make it simple to get to the piano—or to whatever I want to keep consistently in my life.

It is not willpower but habit that makes things happen. And to create those habits, we must create a system. Ask yourself, what is a habit that you want to create consistently in your life? Try to start with something very small. Do it for twenty-one days, immediately after an existing habit. Once you keep it up for those three weeks—which I guarantee will go quickly—you can add more time. The key is to stick with that initial small chunk of time, perhaps about one-tenth of what you could actually do, until you establish the habit.

Don't overdo it. Keep it light and fun.

SOMETHING TO TRY WHENEVER YOU'RE READY:

- Do you have any habit or routine that you failed to keep in the past? Write it here:

_____

_____

_____

» Why do you think it was difficult to keep up? It was (too hard/too long/boring/no time/lack of motivation/not useful/ not prioritizing enough/no reason or other reasons):

_____

_____

_____

» Would you like to try it again, this time with a much smaller chunk of time? Keep it ridiculously small, such as opening up a book and reading for 3 minutes in order to build a reading habit. Your new time goal: every day for . . .

_____

- Do you have a new habit you'd like to add in your life? Write it here:

  _____

  _____

  _____

  » What existing activity/habit would it make the most sense to do this activity after? After doing

    _____

1. Try it for 3 weeks (21 days) but not longer than 10 minutes each day.

2. Share your challenge with your family and friends today.

3. Create 21 boxes on a sheet of paper with each date and put it someplace where you can't miss it.

4. Mark an X each time you do the habit challenge.

5. If you miss a day, tear up the paper and start over. The goal is to do that habit for 21 consecutive days. Remember, it is okay to fail now and then. I know eventually you will succeed.

6. Celebrate when you finish your 21-day challenge!

2

PROCESS AS A GOAL, NOT AN OUTCOME

*O*n a beautiful fall morning in San Diego, I opened up a book of Chopin music in my living room. I had always wanted to start to learn *Andante Spianato and Grande Polonaise* by Chopin. I had learned that, very often, music would find its own season to enter into my life, and this has held true to this day for me. I just have to wait for the right timing to welcome a certain piece to reside with me for a while. On this particular day, finally, this piece visited me and knocked on my door. I felt an excitement growing in me as I played the first page of the slow *andante* section.

I had just finished a big concert tour in Michigan, a summer music festival called *Baroque on Beaver*, where I performed three concerts in a week: playing a solo piano program, one chamber music concert of the *Schumann Piano Quintet*, and finishing with Mozart's A major, K. 488 concerto with a festival orchestra. Even though I enjoyed every minute of the experience, it was an intense week for me. If this were the equivalent of a sporting competition, then I was being asked to do a triathlon: a solo performance of bicycling, then chamber music of swimming, then finishing up with a concerto performance with an orchestra as my final footrace in my musical triathlon. Typically, the more intensive the concerts were to prepare, the sweeter the feeling of freedom I felt after they were over. On this special day, I feel a special freedom as I get to explore something new to learn!

I love these in-between days in my schedule; there's no immediate concert that I need to prepare for, so I can simply spend time with myself to play and discover new music. It is a joy to allow myself to explore and just fiddle around with any repertoire that I want to have fun with on the piano—without any agenda. I am allowed to be clumsy, making all the mistakes there are in the world on the piano, being messy, exploring new sounds, and welcoming any possibility. You know that feeling of the first day of spring when you're a kid, when you have crayons of all colors in your yard and you're there to intentionally make a mess. There are no worries or boundaries in this creation—you're there to have nothing but sheer fun.

> The real joy that I discovered was not about the destination but about the daily act of doing.

That is how I start with any repertoire that I end up performing in my concerts. The first stage of learning is filled with the great excitement of everything new in that honeymoon stage of the fresh relationship with a piece. Then a day or two, maybe a week goes by. Soon the real struggle of the piece, the real journey, starts to set into the practice routine. No more messy playing, no more just goofing around with careless fingering is allowed. I change gears so I can absorb the piece as properly as possible, incessantly altering the way I tackle the repetitions, finding the proper way of playing, the proper technique for each section, while discovering different nuances of tone and a musical voice on each line of the composition. It doesn't mean that this stage of learning is any less exciting than the playful, honeymoon stage, but it is surely different. It is a time to get to know my new musical friend properly after having our first chat at that initial cocktail party.

I am always amazed at how long it takes to learn a piece—actually to understand the piece to a degree that I am able to perform it with a great sense of freedom. Often it feels like a relationship with a person. It takes many months, often years; yet you can never say that you know it for sure, as there is so much more to be learned and to be explored. And of course, I, the person learning the music, am also constantly changing with time, which makes this relationship even more complicated.

I always wished that, once you have learned a piece, after you have good tempo and good technique with proper musical expression memorized well in your brain and fingers, and after you have performed many times in public concerts, you should be able to say that you got the job done. Right? Mission accomplished.

I wish!

The actual reality that I've encountered as a pianist is far from what I thought it would be. The piece, in fact, is NEVER "finished." I can never put a stamp on a piece, saying that "I have got this, and this is done." The piece that I thought I knew often comes to me as raw and new again once I am on a stage. It can feel like a total stranger after putting it aside for a year or two, and new discoveries about how this piece can be expressed are ever-evolving, no matter how much I have practiced or performed it.

> "Never done" means another possibility of learning and discovery. It is rather a relief to know that there is no end.

I used to hate this part of the process. Sometimes it felt like a betrayal. I would ask myself, "How can this piece that I have worked on for six months feel new all over again? Why can't I say I know this piece absolutely if I worked for this long?"

I have to admit that this is still not an easy concept to accept as a truth. I always felt vulnerable onstage, regardless of how much I knew or understood that piece. Interestingly, live performances always gave me something new, something exciting to be discovered. But this became possible only when I allowed myself to feel vulnerable. "Never completely done" meant there was more room for another possibility.

The feeling of vulnerability in live performance is a miniature exercise of accepting life as it is or me as who I am. I've come to learn the lesson that part of existing as a human being is to accept the ever-changing progress of who we are and what is.

After failing a piano audition miserably during my doctorate years at Indiana University, I spoke with one of my mentors, David T. Bremer. I was mad, somewhat disappointed, but mostly sad. I told him how much I had worked and how much I'd wanted this to turn out in the way I had wished.

> Live performances always challenge me as an exercise in life—to accept who I am and to accept how things are right now.

"Why did this happen?" I said. "I worked so hard! You can't even imagine how much I practiced for this."

He didn't nod or give me a comforting look. He simply spoke two sentences while giving a rather dry, blunt, and serious look.

"Don't ask about 'why,' ask 'what now?' Your job now is to go back to school and resume your practice."

That was all he said. No explanation. No babysitting. Then he told me that if I found a solution, to call him back. I thought he didn't understand my situation and didn't care about how I felt, but I did what he advised without really understanding where he was coming from. I actually didn't have to call him back. I internally knew that I just needed to accept it and move on. After his passing five years ago, I often think about that conversation we had. I still thank him for that wisdom he shared, every time I face a challenge in my life. I hear his voice in my head. *Are you asking "why" or "what now"?*

I now understand his intention at that time. He was turning my attention to make an action to do something *now*, not contemplating a negative chain of thought. He was simply redirecting my energy from the past to be in the now. I've found myself many times wondering why certain things happened to me, hearing my own voice complaining and whining. Of course, the answer always came back with silence or no reasonable answers. A life, after all, does not come with a manual, nor does it arrive with a preset, rational reasoning. I needed to simply accept whatever is and move forward.

> Always ask, "WHAT NOW?"

Thinking about "what now?" is about being present in the moment, accepting the current situation, whether good or bad, and mentally preparing to take action. Every step of learning a new piece of music, or learning anything new, must come with the daily accepting of what's true NOW, and the ever-changing discovery of a new relationship. No more saying "I used to know this piece well," or "Why can't I play this piece well yet?" or "Why did my memory slip on that section of the piece after I practiced for months?" Instead, I started to replace that with "What should I practice NOW, at this hour?" or "What is the challenge spot today?" or "What kind of strategies can I apply in this tricky section?" These turned out to be much more helpful options for me.

When I sit down at a piano, I now think about the process of learning—getting to know the piece, the discovery process inherent to each step, the ups and downs, the struggle of challenging sections in terms of technique, and the agony of memorizing. I think about that first day that I found it easier to play, or the day I first performed it in public.

> We have to learn to accept the ever-changing process of who we are now and who we are becoming.

This journey has been full of daily discovery of musical treasures, such as a new finding of tones and nuances of a section, or fresh layers of feelings or harmonic languages. Even the pain of learning a piece gave me joy.

While a concert day may seem like a final destination or finish line from other people's perspectives, for me it is a day to celebrate the process. It is like a rest stop on a road trip, getting some fuel and snacks along the way. It is surely exciting to share the piece and perform, but that is not the final destination for the piece. The journey is ever ongoing—onstage or offstage, before or after a concert. What I have learned is that, as soon as I accepted that the daily journey of the process IS my goal, things began to feel easier and lighter. I want to continually play the piano. Not to arrive at a destination and be done with it, but just simply to keep playing, feeling this joy of creating music all the time—both in concert and in daily practice. I've found the line has blurred between the two.

> The goal is to continue doing the work that you love every day, not get to a destination and be done. The secret is to love the process.

Now that I have come to see performing as no different from practicing, I feel excited to find new beauty in what I play each day, and even adore the daily grind and the occasional pain of repetition. I feel relieved that there is no shortage of this hunting for treasures as long as I play, as long as I show up and I sit down at the piano. I love the fact that we—all of us—are always *becoming*. Without judgment or the threat of an expiration date—fearing we might "spoil" before we finish. I know I will feel stuck and fail many times, but that is just part of the big adventure.

What is your journey of becoming? Are you set on a result as your ultimate goal? Are you asking yourself *why* certain projects of yours are not working in a way you wished?

Or are you asking yourself what to do now? Have you ever thought about the process of becoming as a goal in and of itself?

Try to discover the joy of doing the work rather than focusing on the final outcome. I encourage you to toy around with this idea of accepting the most boring process of your daily task as an ultimate goal. For me, this was a game changer. I am slowly starting to understand the beauty of the journey—that it's about being fully in the NOW.

 ## SOMETHING TO THINK ABOUT WHENEVER YOU'RE READY:

- When is the last time you asked yourself "why" something happened to you? Can you change that question to "what to do now"? How does it change your perspective of the situation?

- Think about the following sentence:

  » I love doing _____. My wish is that I continue loving doing _____ every day throughout my life. I enjoy the daily aspects of this activity, just like I do walking on a hiking trail, smelling flowers, or looking at and appreciating the vast variety of scenery or gorgeous mountain ridges. The goal here is to enjoy the act of walking on the path, not to arrive at the destination and be done.

3

EFFICIENCY WINS OVER AMOUNT OF TIME

I often visit New York City for concerts and musical projects. There is my to-go studio, where I rent a decent piano hourly for my practice. As everything in New York is pricey, I typically have to pay between $25 and $30 an hour to practice on a piano. (To clarify, I mean not to perform, not to give a lesson—I am simply paying this fee to practice alone.) I must say that probably my best practice sessions take place during those one or two expensive paid hours, as I am doing my very best to make sure every minute is not wasted. I plan exactly what and how I will practice in advance. A twenty-or-thirty-minute walk to the studio from my hotel gives me time to mentally and meticulously prepare myself for the next two hours of practice. It's always an interesting experience for me to learn a new perspective on time and efficiency.

When you know that you have only two hours to do something, you've paid for those two hours, and you can't do that activity at any other time in the day, something shifts within you. You really consider that usage of time. You know you can't waste those hours. You have to find ways to maximize what you can achieve within that time frame, so you prepare mentally and intellectually. So often, I use my "free" time without giving much thought about how to spend it, compared to those precious paid-for hours of practice. It is an interesting mind game for me, when I consider the implications of that experience. How could I apply that efficiency mindset even when I don't have to pay for it?

"How long do you practice?"

This might be one of the most frequently asked questions I get from those curious about how I came to where I am now. I can never accurately tell people the exact answer, as it seems to be always changing throughout my life. But I have often asked that question of myself. How long is enough? How can I know enough is enough?

During my high school years, I was told that except when you are eating, sleeping, or going to the bathroom, you should be playing the piano. I did not take that advice literally, nor could I make that happen. Even if I always told myself (fairly decidedly), "I will try to make practicing the piano the only thing I do during my summer break," that summer break with non-stop practice sessions never came. Every night during the break, I would say to myself, "I will start practicing tomorrow." But that tomorrow somehow always disappeared into a fantasy. I thought, quite ambitiously, that I would do seven or eight hours of practice each day back in high school, but I only got to do a range of two to five hours max regularly.

> Time is money. When I had to pay to practice, something changed in me. I started to think more about HOW I would spend that time.

My longest record of practicing must have been around six hours, which occurred during my doctorate years. Even then, I stuck to this schedule only for a very short time. Out of curiosity, I was experimenting with challenging myself, rather than making it a routine. I have to admit that there were some fellow pianists in those university years who actually were able to achieve those superhuman hours of practice daily, and practiced all night, sleeping a bare minimum number of hours. This proved to me that such devotion was not just a myth but actually could be pulled off. These people came out of the practice room at six in the morning with a book of Beethoven sonatas in their hands, saying they had learned and memorized a whole sonata during the previous night. Since I was surrounded by those fanatical musicians, I always thought I was never practicing enough—the constant voice of judgment in my head never failed to remind me of that.

During the past decade of my life as a professional pianist, after moving away from the environment of academia, I've discovered something significant for myself: the fact that I *was* doing enough. Even when I've practiced only one or two hours a day or even less, that was just the right amount of time, as I might have only that amount of energy or focused mind that day. I've come to learn that being gentle on myself with regard to how long I practice has allowed me to practice more efficiently when I do. It is not the *amount* that matters, but *how* I practice.

Before I tackle my piece on a piano, I think of several strategies to solve the difficult parts in advance. Maybe that could be dancing or singing along with the piece, or just drills with separate hands, or simply running through the piece to get a sense of the overall picture. While professional athletes have coaches to help them train to reach their maximum performance, guiding their daily workouts and drills, professional musicians

> It is not the amount that matters, but more importantly, *how* I do the task.

are expected to be their own coaches, and to make sure they follow through on practice skills, executing them every day, religiously. In this regard, musicians are required to wear both hats—that of a performer but also that of a coach. The hours that I spend at a piano are not only physical, but they also have a lot to do with the mental and intellectual *thinking* side of music, which requires problem-solving skills.

I have always wished that I could have a coach, every time I practice. About 250 years ago, that was actually a trend. Aspiring musicians knocked on masters' doors and announced they wished to learn something from the master, while offering also to clean their house for them. In the modern reality of the twenty-first century, I had to train myself to be my own coach so I could come up with my own strategies for each practice session. In fact, I have learned that this coaching skill is part of the fun. You get to be a coach and a player at the same time. Sometimes you need to give your athlete a drill to practice; other times, another form of mental training might be needed. Simply showing up and doing a drill won't work. As a coach, you need a good strategy and plan beforehand to make it work. This is a common characteristic of musicians; we are trained to practice alone, even from the first lesson. That solo practice is not an automatic talent, but a learned skill.

Those days that I have the best practice are when I plan in advance and create a detailed hourly schedule in the morning. I have the best outcome when I know what my one goal of the day is and what my one practice goal of each hour is. I write out what I hope to be doing each morning for each hour of practice and, when I sit down at the piano, I write the one goal of each session in my practice notebook. This is actually not as rigid as you would think, as you can also write as many breaks as you wish into your planning. What I believe is valuable is that you get a better or more precise sense of time by doing this planning exercise, and knowing how long it takes for you to get ready, to eat, to take a break, or to do a task can be very helpful in terms of this. Actually, in order for me to accomplish two hours of practice, I would need about two and a half or three hours total time, as I know I would like some breaks between those hours. I have learned to schedule more padding of free time between each hour of practice.

I encourage you each morning to try to write out your day's schedule in hourly or thirty-minute blocks, keeping it as detailed as possible, and then to review how it actually worked at night. I hope that what you will learn from this exercise is to have a sense of time for yourself. Then, you can adjust it accordingly. What it will give you by doing this is a scanning of your sense of time. Some things might take longer than you thought, or others may not require as much as you thought, or you would like more efficient usage of one block of time by adding more planning time in advance.

Writing down your hourly plan for the day gives you a focus for each activity you intend to do. Time disappears easily without us noticing. Catch it before it goes away, or at least watch where it goes. "Awareness" of the time is what we practice by doing it.

I find this time blocking is valuable, as it gives me a focus of what I intend to do. With this focus comes a sense of freedom and creativity within each time block, as there is no other work I need to be doing, but to solely home in on one thing.

We are living in a world of multitasking. Even though I still do some multitasking on purpose, such as walking while talking with my mom on the phone or putting on makeup while listening to the radio in Spanish (because I'm trying to learn that language), I truly believe in doing one task at a time for most of my day. I've learned that multitasking basically means you do two things badly rather than one thing well. This is especially true with a task like practicing piano, which requires your whole being to be present and engaged—physically, emotionally, and intellectually. Practicing this exercise of doing one task at a time has helped me navigate other daily obligations. It simply doesn't work to try to practice piano while thinking about what to eat later or who I want to talk to. Each day and each hour, I make a conscious choice of where I want to be and what I want to do.

Even an activity like exercise is something I like to do in silence—for example, focusing on a muscle I am using or on my breathing. I think of this as single-tasking, as opposed to multitasking. While I know there are some opposite theories that suggest using fast-speed music helps our motivation of movement, and I am sure it works for others, I have grown to enjoy the silence in my workouts and the joy of focusing on one thing at a time. My workout times, whether they consist of yoga, weights, or swimming, are my peaceful time for me to meet myself. With my own gentle guidance to focus on breathing or allow the mind to daydream, that void of time, with no interrupting or distracting stimulation, has been a great source of peace.

> Multitasking is doing two things badly rather than one thing well. Simply commit to doing that one thing. It helped me be more creative, happy, and efficient.

Single-tasking actually helps my mind focus when I'm practicing the piano too. I've learned that playing piano requires that my whole being become engaged. Focusing on the one thing you're doing also helps dispel the common misperception that quantity of time practicing is more important than quality. That practice-time myth that I used to have in my youth, back during high school summers when I thought I should be practicing all day except when I was sleeping or eating, was not necessary, and was harmful to my mental well-being. I just needed a good, focused practice that revolved around ONLY that task, savoring each minute. Then, the rest of the time, I could take a break, read, walk, teach, and immerse myself fully in other things. If I work hard on one task, I am then able to rest completely on my break.

I believe this focused approach helps me remain in a state of being in the now, as long as I devote myself to each moment, value it, and remember to savor it. For me, the secret to getting to that point is, as I've said: plan ahead. In the morning, I write down a schedule for the day so I can protect myself from other distractions and focus completely on that *one thing*. Of course there will be moments I am pulled from my focus, but if I plan in advance, I can

> I was able to listen to my own intuition more clearly when I simply did one thing at a time, giving more room for my brain to breathe.

better manage interruptions—and decide what to prioritize in that day and when to do it. For example, looking at my cellphone isn't a distraction until I decide it's a distraction.

What is your *one thing* that you intend to do right now? Do you know? Try to design your day ahead of time and be conscious about what to focus on and what does NOT deserve your focus. If anything, you will learn more about how you spend your time and what you value. Turn on a timer for thirty minutes, shut the world down by setting aside your phone and minimizing other distractions, and simply do that one thing. Awareness of the importance of time comes when you allow yourself to be able to forget time.

SOMETHING TO TRY WHENEVER YOU'RE READY:

Plan tomorrow in advance. It is best if you can even plan for smaller chunks, such as thirty or even fifteen-minute time blocks. Review at the end of tomorrow which activity went as you planned, or which activity took longer or less time than you thought it would. Use a timer when needed for a certain activity so you don't have to worry about keeping track. Try to do one thing at a time without distractions. (Yes, your phone too!) I am curious if that makes you feel differently or how it affects how you spend your day.

CHECK if you accomplished it	TIME	PLAN TO DO
	6:00	
	7:00	
	8:00	
	9:00	
	10:00	
	11:00	
	12:00	
	13:00	
	14:00	
	15:00	
	16:00	
	17:00	
	18:00	
	19:00	
	20:00	
	21:00	
	22:00	
	23:00	

4

FIND WORK AND REST
BALANCE FOR YOURSELF

*R*esearch says that on average, it takes about sixty-six days before a new behavior becomes automatic. Although it depends on each person, the range can be anywhere from eighteen to 254 days for people to form a new habit. I find that it is true for me, too, whenever I try to incorporate a new habit or even a new piece of music. There is a certain amount of time necessary to get that in my system.

Even though sixty-six is not an absolute number for getting a habit established, I do love that structure. There are many habit calendars on the internet that you can easily download. You can start to create a new sixty-six-day habit calendar, drawing an X on each day when you accomplish what you set out to do. I have tried some new workout routines, for instance, such as every-morning stretches or something more diet related like no desserts, or simply playing one piece of music for sixty-six days (hopefully without breaking the chain of doing it initially).

While it seems like a noble concept to establish something in about two months, the reality is that this amount of time can actually feel really long and tedious. I was trying to do daily stretches as the first thing in the morning, but I found that there was always a day where it seemed to be impossible to accomplish it. The exciting idea of keeping one new habit consistently was often tested to skip and move on to the next thing that kept my attention. On those days, I applied my two-day rule that I learned from a filmmaker, Matt D'Avella, which is that I can skip one day, but not two days in a row. That gives me wiggle room to allow myself to fall back if that is how it needs to be, while being gentler on myself. On the second day, however, there is no wiggle room. I simply need to get back on track, no ifs, ands, or buts.

> Although the number 66 might not be the magic number for everyone, I do love how the structure of a 66-day challenge gives me a solid goal.

I often conducted this 66-day habit challenge with my piano students. The challenge can be piano related, such as playing one of their repertoires each day, or a life-related habit, like incorporating ten minutes of daily meditation with the help of a meditation app. Every one of my students reported that this structure helped them be consistent, and being able to put a sticker or X mark on the calendar we shared spurred them on. Having accountability partners that kept track of their progress, which involved sharing their goals and reporting back afterward with each other, was also a great motivator for them to accomplish this challenge.

I find that a visual map of this habit forming is very helpful. I place the map somewhere I can't miss—on the bathroom door or refrigerator, where I can put an X mark on each box of the day. If I end up skipping a day, I know for sure tomorrow I need to be back doing the task by visually seeing that one missing X sign. By having this kind of rule, it was much easier for me to give myself a gentle pat on my shoulder, and tell myself, "I am doing my best. It is okay to fall back today. Let's start again tomorrow."

Finding the balance between being nice to myself yet pushing to be better seems to be an art in and of itself. There will always be an intriguing project that I would like to try, or music that I would like to learn, or books that I want to read, or some new habits that I want to experiment with. Sometimes it feels easy to work all day. Then there are times that I simply want to relax and

> Don't underestimate the value of a visual cue. Simply write down your habit goal and put a huge X on a calendar when you accomplish it. This creates a strangely good sensation that something has been accomplished.

let loose without putting much thought into it—perhaps being lazy and doing nothing, or binge-watching Netflix. It is only natural for us to feel a desire to become better and work hard, yet there is also a need to take a break from our endeavors.

I like the balance of the 6-to-1 ratio. Just like in the Judeo-Christian tradition, you work six days, and rest and worship on the seventh day, the Sabbath. You can also think of it this way: You put out effort for about eighty-five percent of the time, and you rest for the remaining fifteen percent.

Interestingly, I am writing this during the COVID-19 quarantine. I have never thought that I would be forced to have a pause button on my life. None of us did! All of a sudden, it feels as though the world just stopped turning. For me, that meant there was no external push—no concerts scheduled, no other people expecting me to show up and perform. I was left to do everything alone, in silence.

The first week or so, I was feeling stuck, yet quite excitedly at first—finally, I got to have a vacation at home! But then a small, weird thought in the back of my head asked what not having to perform a concert would mean to me as a pianist—without being able to share with others. I was forced to take a break. In a way, it was an upside-down version of the working versus resting ratio; now it was rest for most of the time with little work. Then, after a couple weeks of staying home without any external push, I realized that I had trained to quarantine for my whole life.

> If you push 85%, make sure you fully rest 15%. You will have to find your version of the balance, so you know when to push, and when to unplug. That is an act of art in itself.

Playing piano does not require others to tell me what to do every day. I just do what needs to be done, regardless of whatever is going on in the world. I have found that it is not the external world that propelled me on, but that I was the one who made the decision to move forward with the joy of music throughout my life. I started to create new livestreaming for my YouTube channel, *Funday Live*, and have connected virtually with my audience at 2 p.m. every Sunday to give a live concert.

I started *Funday Live* in March 2020. It would be a lie to say there weren't a couple of times I didn't feel like doing it and was tempted to skip a Sunday, but I kept showing up, keeping the promise I made for myself when I first started—I wanted to do the livestream for at least three months, until I could get back into my momentum of consistency in my life. No, no one asked me to do that. If I stopped, people would have been okay with it and moved on to the next thing. Rather, I did it for myself first. The fact that people might have loved it was a side bonus. The point of the story is that I created a new method and strived to find a way to find consistency in my creative work, even through the turmoil created by the outside world.

I am certain that there *is* something you can do when you feel stuck, when the ratio is upside down, where you are spending eighty-five percent of your time not working and procrastinating and fifteen percent of it doing the work. When you feel you are not going anywhere, stop asking the world to give you a chance. You are the one in charge. Try creating some way to share what you do with the world or with your friends and show up each and every day for at least three months. Let the world help you keep going so you can gain your momentum back.

> Don't forget that you are in charge. Create something that helps you move forward first. Give the world a chance to help you achieve your goal.

I drew a big wall calendar in my room and started to draw an X on each day during COVID-19, for the three tasks that I chose as my priority: 1. practicing piano, 2. moving my body (any form of exercising, even if it was just a stroll to the park), and 3. writing (or reading). This time it was not a 66-day challenge to form a new habit—I simply took it one day at a time, as I didn't know how long this quarantine would last. I thought it would be helpful for me to check the baseline priority with myself.

I can't believe how much that simple visual calendar on the wall helps me stick to my daily tasks. The giant calendar is always there on the way to my bathroom to help remind me, asking me, "Did you move your body yet?" Of course, I never forget to practice piano, but I still give that a top visual priority position on my calendar and cheer when I keep it consistent. I congratulate myself for the tiny steps I make each day as I meet these small challenges.

Surprisingly and a bit strangely, I seem to always look forward to putting a big X on the calendar with my white chalk marker for each day I accomplish my tasks. Scientists have proven that using a checklist benefits the user's mental clarity. I wholeheartedly agree, and I have expanded using this list technique for a variety of purposes. These days, I write many things in a checklist format, such as my task list for

> Use the two-day rule as a way of being gentle on yourself. You need to be the best cheerleader for your own life first.

practice sessions, my repertoire list of musical pieces I need to keep up, the three things that I am grateful for on any given day, and my priorities in terms of the work I need to do each day. My reason for sharing this list with you is simple: It really works. It gives me that extra visual push that I need for myself daily. And I know it will work for you.

But rest, too, is important—which is why I like to keep that on the list as well. More and more, I have come to realize the importance of good rest for my body and mind. Working for and by myself has made this concept very difficult to keep up at times, but I always do my best to be conscious about resting—moving away from the piano and taking time off from whatever I've been doing. Even with the change of routine resulting from COVID-19, including the upside-down ratio of more downtime than work, I have found that while I continue keeping busy, I still need to take the time to draw a line between that work and the importance of recharging. I take more walks, which help me break physically from the piano, for example. I still keep in mind the two-day rule (that it's okay to skip one day, but not two in a row, when keeping a calendar), and I also remember to apply the Sabbath ratio of 6:1 in my balance between work and rest.

> A checklist works well for me. Whatever form it takes, it clears my brain not to overthink and keeps my vision in check.

It is okay to have a day to rest and forget. Once you fully allow yourself to move away from it completely, but don't allow yourself to fall into procrastination quicksand, whatever you are trying to do will have more of a chance to grow into your life consistently.

Be the best cheerleader to yourself first. It is okay to take a break. Let's start again tomorrow. You are doing great.

"VICTORY, VICTORY! V-I-C-T-O-R-Y!"

SOMETHING TO TRY
WHENEVER YOU'RE READY:

- What are 3 things that you want to keep in your life consistently? For me, it is moving or exercising, practicing piano, and reading or writing. What are yours?

  1. _____

  2. _____

  3. _____

- If you go to the internet and search "66-day habit challenge," you should be able to find many types of 66-day habit calendars available for you to download for free. Print one of those and start your ONE habit challenge today! Put that paper somewhere visible. You can always apply the two-day rule when needed. Just don't skip two days in a row!

5

THE TURTLE WINS THE RACE OVER THE RABBIT

I always enjoyed the fable of the slow and steady turtle racing against the more competitive, faster rabbit from my childhood. My storybook had vivid cartoon images of these two characters. One summer day, the boastful rabbit, who bragged about how fast he could run, was challenged by the turtle to have a race. The turtle walked with his typical steady and painstakingly slow pace throughout the entire race. From the rabbit's perspective (and no doubt most novice readers would agree), the outcome of the race would be too obvious to bother trying his hardest, or even trying very hard at all. But when the rabbit takes his time to do other things along the way—sniffing flowers and eating snacks—he realizes the turtle is about to cross the line first. Even though the rabbit runs as fast as he can toward the finish line, the turtle crosses first and wins the race.

I always wondered why the rabbit did not cross the finish line first and *then* do the other things he wanted to do. Or better yet, why did the turtle challenge the rabbit to this race, even though it seemed obvious the rabbit had the superior ability? Was the turtle not afraid of looking stupid? Wasn't it obvious that the rabbit's natural talent would propel him over the finish line first?

> Life is so much more complicated than simply categorizing someone as having a magic solution of "talent." What we don't see very often is the real effort of "persistence."

This fable is applicable to the world of music. I am often asked about how much I believe in musical talent. Surely one of the most frequent comments I have received at my concerts is "You are so talented!" We are living in a society where young prodigies are praised, and everyone else wishes that they, too, had been born with some magic solution in their DNA—such as musical talent. And if there's a chance that someone seems to have some sort of profound mystical ability, we say they have "talent," as if one individual simply has it and others simply don't.

More than any other field, music is the one area where people believe in this magical ability. As a teacher myself, I have seen many young children who have a great sense of rhythm or fast finger movements or wonderful musical phrasing without needing my guidance. Just like the fast rabbit in the story, they are such naturals—so gifted— that it might seem obvious to me that they will do well as musicians throughout their lives, even as wonderful professional musicians, *if they run as fast as they can from now on, and do so steadily.*

Interestingly, those children who seem to have great intuition in certain aspects of music often lack the qualities of persistence and discipline. I am not entirely sure why this is so, but maybe it is because those musical abilities came to them too easily and they did not have to work at it. These students often wait until the last minute to practice certain sections, often just relying on their own ability to play music, rather than taking on the humble attitude of wanting to learn and improve.

When observing the trajectory of many musician friends of mine, as well as that of my own students, the very obvious race between a fast rabbit and a slow turtle does not seem all that obvious anymore. I am reminded of a student of mine who did not seem to have particularly strong musical aptitude at first, but who nonetheless became a beautiful professional pianist. And then there is the promising musician friend from my arts high school, who won a majority of the competitions and showed all outward signs of obtaining a promising future as an amazing musician, but who ended up losing interest and abandoning music entirely.

To my astonishment, I have started to wonder what talent actually is. Do we even have a talent in music or any other field? What is it then?

Do I believe in talent in music? This is actually not a simple question to answer anymore. I believe that musical ability needs to be uncovered over a long period of time, probably a lifetime. You may love music—which is the one thing I believe that IS something (a talent, perhaps) you have without training—but you need a lot of fuel to keep running on the music "track" in life. Let's call this fuel "persistence."

> I believe that any ability can be developed over a long period of time. A lifetime marathon.

This persistence is something that you can cultivate and learn. When this persistence is joined with deliberate practicing, which includes a student's ability to analyze and correct themselves more intellectually and cognitively, along with efficient practice methods and helpful feedback from good instructors, these ingredients finally start to make sense.

Developing your own teacher inside you, being able to correct, and being aware of what is going well or not— metacognition—is critical for any skill development.

I believe that everyone has an inner musician that needs to be awakened. If someone were to ask me what formulas would determine whether someone could become a professional musician, I would say their success could be based on these four factors:

1. Their love of music.

2. Ability to keep going, to persist, no matter what obstacles, lulls, or challenges may arise.

3. Eagerness to improve, which would include deliberate practice on their own, and guidance from instructors providing strong feedback.

4. Developing the metacognitive ability to observe oneself objectively.

All of the above factors can be developed and nurtured with good training, especially the second two. I believe that it is true in other fields, too. Let's say I commit to learning something new and I persistently work at it with a good instructor (the locating of which sometimes requires good luck and persistence as well!). If I keep practicing it every day with a passion, I bet I will be so good that, after ten or twenty years, people might tell me, "You are so *talented*!" Then I might smile and think to myself, "That is so true. I developed my talent on my own, over time."

So why did that turtle challenge himself, even when the race seemed so clearly unfavorable to him? My answer for that is simple—I bet the turtle did not care what others would think, and that it was just another step that he wanted to take, to make progress for himself. He simply found the joy of each step, taken at a steady pace. He had a knack for working hard and employed the admirable qualities of persistence and determination to his advantage. Each steady step was filled with the rewarding sense of moving forward. He had found the joy of improvement, not to show off to the rabbit with, but to prove inwardly to himself that he could achieve the goal.

Let me ask you: Is there anything in your life you think is too late to start learning? Is there any area that you believe you are not talented in, but you love doing that activity? Then *do it*, regardless of what your assumptions about your potential may be. Start, commit to regular practice, and keep going. Be like the turtle and forget about whether others are faster than you are. Make a commitment to keep moving. Perhaps you could try the 66-day challenge we discussed in the previous chapter, as a way to form the daily habit of practice. The key is that you keep doing it for yourself and forget the speed at which you progress.

> Find the joy of improvement and do it for yourself, not for others or to show the world.

This student of mine, whose name is Erik, came to start taking piano lessons when he was 63 years old. His goal? To rock at piano when he goes to a retirement home when he is about 85 years old and entertain everyone living there with him. Into his fifth year of playing piano, he is enjoying this turtle-step of playing piano every day, always full of joy and with a smile on his face.

Forget the rabbit and the other people.

Just start moving. Take that first step into your passion today.

SOMETHING TO THINK ABOUT WHENEVER YOU'RE READY:

What is it that you always wanted to learn and would love to do, but haven't started yet because you think it is too late or you're discouraged as you think you don't have the talent for it?

» I would love to learn how to _____.

» Find an instructor to help you (perhaps through an internet search), and do this NOW.

» Make that first call today for the first appointment, or simply to ask a few questions.

» Find YouTube videos on how to do that activity . . . and start NOW.

» Be motivated . . . NOW.

» Make a decision to commit to your chosen activity and follow through with it.

6

WATER BOILS AT THE
100-DEGREE C MARK

*S*itting down at the piano, I opened a book called *Eight Concert Etudes* by a contemporary Russian composer, Nikolai Kapustin. I have been working on one of these etudes for a month now, but I still don't feel like I am making progress. The tricky independent-hands movement, paired with a complicated jazzy rhythm and a dense harmony, seem to make the advancement for me much slower than it has been with other pieces. I repeated the same four measures over and over. Not much progress. After fifteen minutes, I decided to change the rhythm and articulation and repeated it twenty more times. This particular section will be pretty tough to sort out, I thought. I would probably need to tackle it more intensively each day, every day, for some time. I wrote the following sentence in my practice journal as a reminder:

Repetition works.

The journey of learning a piece of music often feels like walking in a cave without so much as a headlight. The daily practice often feels like the piece is not improving or going much further, with no way of knowing how long this feeling of not moving forward will last. The only thing that sustains me in dark periods like this is the belief that I am making progress—even without much in the way of evidence or any substantial sense of improvement.

I am fairly familiar with this uncomfortable feeling by now, much like a sense of stale water lacking a current. At the same time, I also know that there *is* a current underneath—the forward current that I am creating each day by practicing. Even if I don't feel it, I trust that it's there.

The spotlight and the splendid look of a chandelier in a concert hall often make audiences forget this daily mundane struggle of pianists' lives behind the curtain. The joy of sharing music and being able to perform pieces with the utmost fluency are only possible because of this everyday grind of working on a piece, with the reminder that "I am making progress" to oneself. I always wished that I could say that daily practice is so much fun.

> Repetition does work. How many times did you actually repeat before you gave up? The key is not to stop, and to believe you are making progress.

While that sentence is widely true to me at its core meaning, it is certainly not an amusement-park kind of entertainment. It is the sort of enjoyment that you feel when you take a step closer toward what you love—a much deeper, more complex, and very rewarding kind of fun.

A great musician friend of mine once told me that practicing his flute was like a relationship with a loved one. I could not agree more. It is not about how you *feel* about practicing piano, it is about what you *do* about what you love. Despite how I feel, I show up and exercise my love of music by doing something about it and by playing piano. More often than not, if there is a feeling of initial resistance to practicing, it quickly fades away once I sit down and play the first note. It is a life-long relationship that I have cared for and cultivated.

Everything worthwhile takes time and deserves patience, especially the things we treasure. Some days are harder than others, but I tackle them anyway. Just as an elderly couple does their daily chores for each other, and has done so for many years, I show up each day and keep evolving with practicing and making music on the piano, regardless of how I feel at the start of each day.

Luckily, the most rewarding part about playing piano and practicing each day is the fact that I am the one who receives the most benefit from it. By showing up, by practicing each day, I receive and absorb the magical energy of music, a daily dose of feeling rejuvenated and renewed.

> Moving forward is not easy. Doing is not easy. But you do, because you care. Because you love it. Actions speak louder than words.

And then, that day comes. All of a sudden, out of nowhere, I can play a piece with much more ease and fluency. The section I had been pushing through for months seems to work magically. What happened? Did something change overnight? Am I dreaming or something? With such a delightful surprise, I would say, the water is finally boiling, as it has reached 100 degrees!

That is right. The water would not do anything until it reaches that final degree. Not 97, not 99. But 100 degrees Celsius. (Likewise in Fahrenheit, water doesn't boil at 208 or 210, but at 212—not a smidgen sooner.) During each day of pushing forward without feeling much was happening, I was actually collecting one more degree—to the point that finally I *would* be able to feel it. I finally reached a degree of improvement that was clear to me.

Let me use the analogy of stairs to describe this. Once I reach a certain level of mastery with a piece of music, it is not like I can take a step back down the next day. No, my playing stays in that general improved level—stays on the stairstep I reached the day before. How comforting that is! The only thing I have to remember during my daily practice is that I *believe* that I am making progress, because I AM!

I have to say, it took a while for me to finally accept this concept, believing it to be a firmly rooted reality. It is a similar process with learning a new language. When I was about eighteen years old and living in Korea, I remember wondering if I would ever be able to speak English comfortably in my lifetime. The daily practice, memorizing foreign combinations of vocabulary, and the unfamiliar sounds of this foreign language, English, seemed far beyond my reach. Fast-forward to now. My English may not be perfect, but I am writing this book in English and I have my own podcast in English as well. Am I comfortable with it? Yes.

I won't stop practicing before I experience the day when I feel ease. The joy that comes with that can't compare with anything else. Practice and wait with excitement while doing the work.

In addition, I am now actually learning Spanish with the hope of performing in Spanish-speaking countries in the future. I feel the same way about Spanish as I did about English when I was eighteen—uncomfortable and raw. The difference now? When I reach a certain degree with my daily practice of studying my Spanish, I know for sure I will be fluent one day. Just a matter of time and my persistence.

You see, you mustn't stop because you cannot feel your progress. All along, you have been putting a drop in that bucket you are trying to fill. Or, to stick with the boiling-water metaphor, you might be at the 99-degree mark the very moment before you give up. Just one more push, and you could be feeling success! I suggest you keep doing what you're doing, whatever that may be. I assure you that the day will come when things will feel different than they did the day before, all thanks to your persistence.

It is not magic. It's simply a logical conclusion from your persistent efforts.

All you need each day is *a belief* that you are making progress. Huge progress, in fact.

 ## SOMETHING TO THINK ABOUT WHENEVER YOU'RE READY:

I love *(write one activity)* _____.

It takes time and effort! Often, I am not always motivated to

_____.

» I do it anyway.

» I don't feel progress.

» I do it anyway.

» I believe I am making some progress.

» I do it anyway.

» I don't feel like doing it today.

» I do it anyway.

» Today I feel good about this.

» Good job, I do it anyway.

» Continue!

I promise you that you are moving forward, and you will feel the progress soon. Just don't stop.

Love is what you DO regardless of how you feel.

WALTZ OP. 64, NO. 2 BY FRÉDÉRIC CHOPIN

*C*hopin is regarded as a "poet of the piano." He is considered to be the inventor of the Romantic piano sound as well as the originator of the technical approach on piano still in use today.[2] If you are a pianist, the music of Chopin is something you live with your entire life.

I remember the first time I encountered Chopin's "Black Keys" etude in my teenage years, thinking it was the most otherworldly sound that I'd ever experienced. Soon I figured out that, underneath that beauty, there were many technical challenges required for one to play Chopin well. Chopin's music has been my companion from youth, and I continue to look forward to sharing more of Chopin onstage for others, or simply in my living room for myself. His music has an ethereal power that one can't deny.

What I find fascinating about the music of Chopin is that its language is universal. Even if you've never heard of Chopin, something about his music draws you in and has you gravitating toward its sound. Love is expressed with such sensitivity, yet there is also the idea of a conflict expressed—something that's both happy and sad, smiling yet

---

2 If you'd like to read more about Frédéric Chopin, I recommend the book *Fryderyk Chopin*, by Alan Walker.

crying, and so on. When Chopin first arrived in Paris from his Polish homeland in 1831, his ability at the keyboard was sensational among his accomplished artist peers and Paris high society. Even though he made Paris his home, he continued to live as a Pole in exile rather than as a Parisian. His longing for the sounds and the rhythms of Poland formed the basis of many of his compositions.

I visit Korea at least once a year to visit my family, and just to be around the culture and food that I grew up with. I can't imagine being unable to visit my beloved Korea again in my lifetime, as Chopin was unable to do. That would create a huge hole in my heart that couldn't be filled in any other way. Maybe that sorrow in all of Chopin's compositions is rooted deeply in the longing for his homeland.

Chopin's Waltz Op. 64, No. 2 in C-sharp minor is not intended to be a dance, but it has an adaptation of dance rhythm in its left-hand movement. There are running and circling motions in the right hand that keep that melancholy mood of the piece, while the left hand dances along the keyboard. At some point in the piece, you see a little spot of sunshine peeking through the window, where it allows you a soft smile. The piece expresses some conflicted ideas throughout. You are happy but sad. You are saying no, but at the same time you are hinting yes. You are smiling, yet your eyes are crying.

This fascinating piece of music, Waltz Op. 64, No. 2, may make you miss your home, may remind you of the time that you had your first love, or may make you miss your mother or another loved one. It touches that soft spot in our hearts.

I can't wait to take this journey with you.

Please go to my podcast, *Journey Through Classical Piano*, and listen to it on Season 1, Episode 4. I hope to meet you there. Please take your time.

To listen to the piece and learn more about it, scan here ▶

MOVEMENT #2

Guard Your Mind and Keep Negativity at Bay

1

DON'T LET OTHERS DUMP TRASH IN YOUR MIND

I couldn't hold back my tears any longer, so I phoned a dear friend to talk about the negative review I had just received. My friend was in charge of a large music organization in San Diego, and I trusted his professional opinion. I called him because he'd been at that concert too, and had congratulated me afterward.

At the reception after the concert, my friend told me that he absolutely enjoyed the concert, saying the intimate setting from both the music making and my presentation were elegant, and were a refreshing way to connect with twenty-first-century audiences. On the phone that day, he said he was equally puzzled by the negative review, and added, "Don't even worry about it."

He reminded me that we never know what the real story is with critics—they could have had a bad day or maybe were suffering from indigestion prior to the concert. Who knows? I was so disappointed when I read that review, however, because I was so happy with how the concert went. I was walking on a happy cloud thinking about that concert; I was fully present, feeling a strong connection among the audience, me, and the music. That kind of fulfilling concert as a pianist comes by rarely, even if I aim to nail it like that every time. That's why my heart jumped quickly when I saw that review pop up on my computer from our local paper, but my initial curiosity took an immediate and dramatic downturn. I couldn't believe what I was reading. It seemed as though this critic had attended a different concert than the one I gave. My carefully selected repertoire that was meant to connect me with the audience was apparently not serious enough for his taste, and the personal talk onstage that I'd intended as a way to break the barrier between me and the audience became a meaningless transition to him; he preferred a standard presentation of a typical classical piano recital. How could one person have interpreted things so differently than I had?

It took at least three or four days for me to brush off that negative article—a bit longer than usual for these kinds of things. I murmured to myself, "Gosh, I let this one to get me. Shame on me." Once I got back to myself, I was reminded this is the world that I had been living in all along. There are not only fans and supporters but also people who are pessimistic and naysayers. Over my years of training as a pianist, I always managed

> I have a choice: either giving power to negativity to affect my mind or throwing it away.

to dodge these shots of negativity by not entering too many competitions and avoiding teachers who tend to criticize more than encourage. Despite the fact that competitions lure aspiring young musicians with golden tickets that wave at them with promises of grand futures as performing artists, I also saw the dark underbelly of that promise.

Many musician friends of mine who didn't win a competition fell into a track of "I will never be good enough and I better start selling coffee instead." Not that working at a coffeeshop is a bad thing, but they say it to mean they're thinking about dropping their music—merely because they failed to meet someone else's judgment and viewpoints. As far as competitions go, only 0.00001 percent of people make that slim cut that will provide them with "elite" status. Even if they make it, they have to keep competing against the world to prove they are worthy of being listened to and are better than their competitors.

I have to admit that I am a weak person. I know my weakness well, and one of them is that I can't thrive in that negative-feedback-only environment. Some may, but I can't. I grew up in positive surroundings. Every time my mother looked at me, she told me she loved me, and when she was near, she always put her hand reassuringly on my shoulder. My nanny would dance along with my piano playing with a gentle smile on her face. I sang songs with my full heart without worry of judgment from others; I was a happy kid with music all around me, and the people around me were mostly gentle and content. I knew I could not endure a harsh teacher who did not encourage students. I was eager to improve my piano skills with constructive feedback, but not with harsh criticism or personal insults. I intentionally avoided that kind of teacher in my education. I researched potential teachers in advance and wrote letters to other fellow students to learn about teachers beforehand to minimize the risk of getting stuck with a private teacher who was harsh and critical.

In music institutes, for some weird reason, we find those types of negative-mindset teachers more easily than in other fields. They would throw books to the corner, saying the music they just heard sounded like garbage, and one needs to practice much more than they are already doing—perhaps even more than six hours a day! Students were never good enough or concert-worthy. I knew that competitions with fellow musicians would have slowly eaten up my soul, and I knew I needed that soul to keep enjoying and expressing music with passion. I learned to avoid that kind of environment whenever I had a choice. I did not enter competitions except on very rare occasions, and those five I did enter were smaller concert-type competitions for fun. I focused on my own studies, concerts for real audiences, working on my study with my piano teachers at the university even during my master's and doctorate years. I enjoyed the conversations I had with amazing musicians and mentors. Not to prove anything, but simply to grow in music and share with others.

I was lucky that I did not have to recover from losing competitions or live with the side effects of winning them. I was lucky that I did not have to get over harsh words from negative teachers and come back for more criticism week after week. I was lucky that I did not have to fight against my own voice in my head saying I was not good enough every time I played piano. And yet, the musical world I am living in, the path I chose to take, is not that soft. I still face tough critics writing about my concerts. I still read negative comments posted under my YouTube videos, saying my practice tips are useless or giving a thumbs-down on my performance videos. And I still fight against my own negative thoughts popping up every now and then in my mind.

> Avoiding negativity is not a sign of weakness, but wisdom. No need to fight against. Simply don't go there.

The more I exposed myself to the world to connect with people through my music, the more I increased the possibility and frequency of hearing this kind of negativity, yet I knew that I could not simply live in a sterile lab space. If I were to tuck myself away and play piano in my practice room to avoid the comments, I would be going against my passion for connection through music. I just have to accept the fact that I will always be surrounded by both positive and negative feedback. We all are.

And we all have a choice.

I look at my choice this way: Either I give power to negative thoughts and people, or I simply hold my chin up and keep smiling, minding my own business, which is about creating beauty in this world with music, with the goal of reaching one person at a time. No one, simply no one, has a right over my life, nor my choices within it.

I have learned that avoidance is not a sign of weakness. It is wisdom. Avoiding is much easier than meaningless bloody fights against those toxic thoughts. So, I choose to avoid. Simply look away, stop listening, delete quickly, and toss it in the trash. No need to respond or give any power to that thought or opinion. This is very different from the way we respond to constructive feedback from our fellow musicians and friends that we trust and rely on.

After that bad review that caused my tears, one of my wonderful mentors and friends, Allen Brown, told me that "If someone came into your house and dumped a huge bag of trash in your living room, what would you do? Would you accept that kind of behavior? No! It is the same thing with your mind. Don't let others dump trash in your mind."

I smiled. *Yes!*

Let's guard our minds first.

SOMETHING TO THINK ABOUT
WHENEVER YOU'RE READY:

- When was the last time you gave power to another person's negative thoughts? How did it make you feel?

- The next time you feel like you are giving another person's negative thoughts and opinions energy, think about these ideas:

  » Believe that those words are toxic for you.

  » Physically separate yourself from the source if you can, delete it, and do some other positive activity that can help you forget about it.

  » Don't talk about what was said with others, or as little as possible if you can, because, by doing this, you still give it a chance to live in your head longer.

  » Avoid all future interaction with that negative person.

  » Imagine you have an eraser in your mind and believe that you can simply erase that thought. Try to visualize it.

  » If you can't avoid the person physically, simply DO NOT GIVE POWER to that negative voice; do not permit it to harm your mind. It is trash that you need to throw away. Believe that you can choose how to direct your mind.

  » Listen to music or try yoga. Breathe in and out, then smile.

2

DEALING WITH THE
MONSTER IN YOUR HEAD

*I*n November 2005, at Auer Hall at Indiana University, I was performing Schumann's Fantasy Op. 17 for my master's degree recital. Auer Hall has some of the best acoustics I have ever experienced, and of course, I was playing on "Harold," a nine-foot Steinway piano. Indiana University is hailed as one of the best music universities in America; they have at least eight or nine different gorgeous nine-foot concert Steinway pianos in one facility, from both New York and Hamburg. They all had unique characteristics and their own names—Georgina, Dianne, George . . .

For me, this nine-year-old Harold from New York was the best. He had profound versatility, creating the most sensitive voice but then also the wildest, most thunderous and powerful tone imaginable. He had the perfect combination of youthfulness and a unique, mature tone. Whenever I asked for a certain color from Harold, he always surprised me with more shades and new possibilities for the tone colors. Pianists visualize a certain tone for each passage or note before actually hitting the key, and good pianos like Harold will give pianists a tone that's even better than we could imagine in our heads, which leads to a more sensitive and dynamic music-making experience on the stage. I wasn't sure if I was more excited for this concert or for the opportunity to perform live on Harold. Either way, it was a special concert for me.

I was preparing to audition for the doctorate program, which was my reasoning for this ambitious program to show my potential as a pianist. The Bartok sonata was another piece in the program that required stamina, an accurate rhythmic sense, and a specific nuance of language of Eastern Europe. I felt nervous, but I also felt ready. The first piece, the Haydn Sonata in E-flat major, went beautifully. Harold, as usual, gave me just the right amount of crispness and control that I needed for that piece. I was feeling content, thinking this was going beautifully, having this interesting live conversation with Harold, enjoying every moment.

Then, in the first movement of the Schumann Fantasy, just at the beginning of the second theme, all of sudden my left hand jumped to a key that didn't seem to be the right note. I thought I'd gone to the right key, but the music that followed with the right hand did not make sense. The coordination of my hands didn't find the right musical path to continue with that progression. "Oh, no . . ." The world stopped. There was no sound from me or the audience. Everyone seemed to be holding their breath. I was onstage, alone with Harold, stuck in that transition. It felt like I was having an out-of-body experience. You know, one of those experiences that people say they feel when they are about to die or in the moment of a big accident. I could feel my heart jumping out of my body, and my head was spinning. "What do I do?" I thought. "What do I do?"

> We all live with a monster in our head. It won't go away, but we can always find a way to tame it.

I don't have much of a conscious recollection of how I found my way out at that moment, but I managed to jump to the next section of the first movement, and I finished the rest of the thirty-minute-long Schumann Fantasy. But I was not at peace; there was a bloody war taking place in my head. The monster on one side was yelling in a cynical voice, "What is going on? You are so stupid to make that kind of mistake! Will you be able to keep up the good work after that mistake? Hey! There are very tricky sections coming up—you better watch out not to make that mistake again." On the other side, there was an angel with a gentle voice saying, "Hey, you are doing great. Mistakes are a part of the concert, so just keep going." The kind voice reassured me, telling me, "That was good," and "You will forget this soon."

> Talking to the monster in our head is actually interesting. It tells us a lot about ourselves. Eventually, by arguing with them sentence by sentence, we learn how ridiculously silly and unreasonable their talk is.

Both voices, from the monster and the angel, were equally harming my performance. All I wanted to do at that moment was just go to my room and cry my eyes out as soon as the concert was over. I was beaten up by the battle taking place in my head. Watching the video clip of the concert after a week or two (while mostly covering my eyes with my hands), I discovered that the actual mishap wasn't that bad at all. Maybe one or two minutes at max when I was trying to find the transition from the wrong jump. Apparently, my left hand jumped down one octave lower than it was supposed to and threw me out of balance. But when it was happening, it felt like forever. I realized later that the struggle was not the mishap itself, but the mental battle that ensued immediately afterward. After this concert experience, I desperately wanted to find some way to never again have this kind of war in my head during a live performance.

Over the years of performing professionally, I've noticed a pattern that now I can pinpoint more clearly than I could during those university years. There are two sides of me, a monster and an angel, who always like to be wide awake and like to debate—but only during live performances. Not during the rehearsal, not in a greenroom, not in my practice room, but on a stage with an audience present, the monster and angel slowly and quietly wake up from a long nap to have an intense debate in my head, very loudly.

I actually thought that this was only a battle of mine, but it turned out that all of my musician friends of mine agreed they, too, have these mental battles onstage. Being a musician and being a performing artist means that we deal with these dual sides of ourselves and their never-ending battles. Interestingly, I myself was neither an angel nor a monster, but a mere spectator of the battle.

The best live performances for me, even to this day, are the kinds where there are fewer battles in my head. I can't say there is no battle, because there are still and I know there will be always, but I have to say, it has gotten to a point where it is much more predictable and thereby manageable.

Figuring out how to deal with these battles was one of the main reasons for me to start writing my daily journal. It is so simple, but it works. I learned to write all of the monster's thoughts in advance, and I wrote an argument back as an angel for each sentence. Often those negative voices are rooted much deeper. They may represent critical voices of parents, or a kid on a street from our youth, or teachers from the past, the voice of a partner or friend . . .

Where did they come from? I kept track of their history and patterns until I made sense of them, being able to argue back their silliness and unfairness with the voice of an angel. In fact, I don't have to do this arguing; as my staunch defender, my *angel* has to do it.

I also kept count, and I found the ratio was 1:5—that's one monster's sentence countered with five different defense sentences from the angel to match. Then I also wrote positive affirmation sentences, such as "I am creating beautiful music and I am excited to share it with others,"

"I am loved and loving," and "I am enough." Sentences like "There is only one thing I need to do at this time at this very moment. Just be in the moment" served as affirmation and helped me feel grounded.

When my monster spoke loudly in my head during the live performance, the prepared angel argued back in a hurry with a rehearsed script, and I was able to put my attention back to the content of the music—to the emotion of the piece, or harmony, or texture, or rhythm, something about the very moment of music. The battle went on in the background, but eventually I learned not to pay the voices any attention. You would think the angel voice would help me, but in reality, the voice of an angel during a concert is equally distracting to my music making, if I put too much power into that thought. A thought like "Wow, I am doing great" has nothing to do with the very moment of the note I am producing right then and there. However, angels are on my team. I work with them closely beforehand each day, so they, like benevolent lawyers, can rationally argue back.

This is my daily training routine. Just as a soldier does physical training every morning, like sit-ups or push-ups, I do these mental preparations each day. What I have learned, interestingly, is that this is NOT only applicable to performing artists. We all live with monsters in our head. They say bad things to us all

> I am not the voice of a monster or an angel in my head. I am just a mere spectator of their conversations. My job is to let them do their thing and simply put my focus on my work in front of me.

the time. Those negative voices gain more energy and become active when we feel weak mentally—when we don't feel good about ourselves, when we feel vulnerable, or during a life crisis like a job loss or bad health issues or when the weight of our lives presses down on us. Although I can't guarantee victory over every battle, I know this daily tool for me works more positively than not.

I recommend you prepare for your own battles. Write out all of the negative thoughts you might hear in your head, and then argue back with that good angel defender of yours. Make it a practice to *daily* write a list of positive affirmation sentences about the following: Who do you want to be? What are some good characteristics about yourself, including talents? How do you want to create your life, or what positive thoughts would be helpful about the event or day that you are preparing for?

Daily journaling has been my life savior. It strengthens my thought muscle every day. Just like the body, we all lose muscle each day, little by little. So I need a daily maintenance of my thoughts also.

I try to write six positive affirmation sentences each day, every day. When a battle seems out of control, I say these sentences out loud and do it again and again. I must say that the tiger beside you (the negative voice in your head) will never go away, but you will learn how to tame it. Now when I prepare a particular piece of music for a concert, I prepare equally *or more* mentally, away from the piano. For me, this opened a door for me to enjoy my live performances much more and, most importantly, helped me learn about myself better, which has resulted in feeling more joy in my life. I am calmer now, able to accept whatever comes in the moment, and I am not allowing myself to become a victim.

Getting to know more about the monster inside and at the same time giving lots of sustenance to the voice of my angel is like performing a daily dusting routine in my head. It keeps things clean. We should all try this routine, almost like shopping at a health food store for our minds.

SOMETHING TO TRY
WHENEVER YOU'RE READY:

- Make a list and write out all of your monster's thoughts.

  » Then try to analyze the root of each monster's thought. Was it from your childhood? Someone in the past? Just yourself?

  » Write 3 to 5 sentences of great defense—as your angel would—for each of those negative thoughts. Explain why those negative sentences are silly and untrue. (I know it might be difficult, but just be objective and try pretending you're a good lawyer instead of thinking about it too personally.)

- Let's form your affirmation sentences!

  » I am _____
     (your great personal characteristic).

  » I am _____
     (another wonderful character trait of yours).

  » I am _____
     (another wonderful trait of yours).

  » I am _____
     (some character traits you aspire to).

  » I am _____
     (another characteristic you want to express).

  » I am always _____
     (some activity that you like to do).

EXAMPLE

I am passionate. I am compassionate. I always do my best with everything I do. I create beautiful music to heal people and to connect with
people. I am warm and generous. I am a fit and healthy person. I always
care. I am loved and loving. I am content.

> Try to write these affirmation sentences *every day* for at least a
> month and see if that makes any difference to your mind. Try
> saying them out loud. It is very important to physically write
> these instead of typing or simply thinking about them.

3

WINNER'S MINDSET

*D*uring the years at my high school when I was specializing in the arts, as a piano major, I had a piano exam every semester. Jury members were hired from outside for each of these exams. These juries chose the top three pianists, and the winners were given the honor of performing in front of the entire school. That was something every student in a piano major dreamed of and hoped for during the school year.

Freshman year was a tough one for me. I was not coping well with my parents' recent divorce, struggling between my own piano study and the enormous emotional loss of normalcy in my life. On top of that, I also carried a lot of guilt deep down over the financial burden that I must have put on my mom, who had to support me by herself. Private piano lessons were expensive, but much needed for my future. In my first interview with my new piano instructor, Ms. Suk, she mentioned that I could likely qualify to be in the top three pianists at the school one day if I worked hard, and told me that I had a great musical intelligence (which I still don't understand to this day). I honestly thought she was joking. Maybe she was just trying to be nice, sensing my uneasy feeling of the many changes in my life at that time.

I never thought I could achieve the honor of being named in the top three pianists. In my school, filled as it was with serious musicians who had been playing from a young age, those top three always rotated among familiar names. These winning students played cleanly, convincingly, accurately, and, in my eyes, were no doubt worthy of the honor. Although there were minor changes and rotations among the winning names, there was never a winner who was unexpected. Me? No. My past piano position until then always ranged between the ranking of 15 to 25, out of 100 pianists. Achieving a ranking among the top three was something way beyond my reach. I thought I was not bad, but I knew I wasn't the best either.

Making a conscious decision to do the best, and go beyond the best, was the single most important decision I've ever made in my life. It always opens doors to a new me and brings me new opportunities.

When I started piano lessons with Ms. Suk, they were unexpectedly interesting and fun. She'd just come back to Korea from her recent piano studies in Italy and had a refreshing way of approaching music. Surrounded by the current musical education trend in Korea that focused on accuracy and technical excellence, by contrast, Ms. Suk focused on musical expression and finding a suitable musical voice for each piece, which actually resulted in me playing more at ease and also better technically. In her lessons, technique was always a servant to the master of proper or appropriate musical expression. She told me that music always should resemble nature, like a stream running through a mountain—never forced, never artificial, but a natural flow.

I recorded each lesson and listened to them over and over again until I felt like I had learned the concept correctly. I practiced hard in the way she asked me to, and questioned everything about the piano in order to find improved techniques that would lead to better music expression. Piano was my oasis and my sole focus, especially during that turmoil that I was having as a teenager. I really wanted to do my best, crazy best. I didn't know where I would end up going with the piano. I never even thought about exactly what I would do with my music. I was simply committed to throwing all of myself into the piano. I remember making that conscious decision about doing my best after one lesson with Ms. Suk. I felt a renewed energy with her guidance.

Joy and freedom come only after giving everything you have. That is the way to break through another layer of yourself. Once I tasted this level of joy and happiness, I knew I was hooked forever.

The piano exam always took place without a curtain and in an open classroom; the jury members could see who was performing. Then one semester, they thought it would be fairer if they conducted the exam with a closed curtain, so the juries would remain behind the curtain while the students performed. At one piano exam, my number was called out to the jury behind the curtain. I walked into the large, seemingly empty room filled with only a grand piano. I sat down quietly, and I closed my eyes. I let the music lead me, and soon the room was filled with the sound of the piano—and with the quiet existence of the judges behind the curtain. When the piece was over, even though I didn't hear anything from behind the curtain, I still felt a strong connection with the music and the people, without seeing them. I walked out of the room quietly, and the next student walked in.

As I walked back home, I was full of an inexplicable sense of freedom and bliss, a deep connection to both the music and the listeners behind the curtain. It was absolutely a wonderful feeling. Even though I could not see anyone that afternoon, their existence made that performance special and helped me dig deeper into the music in those moments that I played. For me, it wasn't a mere piano exam, but a shared experience of music with anonymous listeners.

One afternoon after that piano exam, I was mopping the floor in my classroom during our regular cleaning time, when one of my best friends ran toward me in a hurry with a big smile on her face. "Jeeyoon, Jeeyoon! Did you see that wall announcement yet? Oh my gosh! You are in the top three pianists!"

Maybe it was the closed curtain, maybe it was the day, maybe it was Ms. Suk's magic teaching wand, maybe it was my hard work, or maybe it was my determination to give it my all . . . I didn't know what exactly the reason was, but ever since that exam, every time I finish a performance of any kind, I feel the very same sensation I felt in that empty room in my high school with listeners behind the curtain—that strong connection to the music, a delight that wells up from deep within me, and then a sense of freedom. A freedom that only comes after giving everything I have up to that point.

> Visualize and imagine that you are already doing excellent work in your task, well beyond your dreams. Don't underestimate your true potential.

That was the first time that I felt I broke one invisible layer of myself with my max efforts. The experience of being able to form a link between my hard work and a certain result has become an inner asset that I have always been able to tap into. This was a new kind of happiness and joy that brought something into my life that I had never experienced before. In many ways, I have to say that I am addicted to the intensity of working hard and feeling free.

One of my students, Patrick, was playing the Chopin Etude Op. 10, No. 1. This was one of his favorite pieces that he wanted to learn, and he was enjoying the process. I love this etude of Chopin; that extension of the right hand with a howling bass melody always reminded me of gorgeous waves in the ocean. When he finally got all the notes well and could play with a consistent medium tempo, I noticed a pattern where he was simply satisfied with his progress and stopped improving—just as I had begun to think he was finally getting into the fun process of learning this piece. I asked him if there were any changes in his daily practice, in the hope of finding a reason for his recent slow progress. He simply said, "Honestly, all I want is just to be able to play this music. I don't think I'll ever play like a professional pianist like Rubinstein or Horowitz. My work with this piece is actually . . . done." Trying to hide my startled look from him, my head was spinning over the words he'd just said.

I'm told that when athletes enter the Olympics, they don't necessarily believe they will win a gold medal. Some Olympic runners' goals might be just getting past the first round—the first cut—or so. Others are simply happy to have the title of Olympic athletes. According to Stan Beecham in his book *Elite Minds*, when athletes win a gold medal, it's never accidental. Top winners have a sharp focus and intensity, as well as a strong belief before the game that they will be the gold medal winners—even during their preparation for the Olympics. Each athlete's training and outcome differs dramatically, depending on whether they believe they can be a gold medal winner, or they simply want to get past the first round.

> The real change and improvement happen at the point of our limit. Without pushing it forward, you will always remain in the same zone without discovering something new about yourself. That is a big loss for the world.

I think this creates an interesting comparison with musicians as well. I suggest that my students practice a piece as if they were an amazing pianist like Rubinstein or Uchida, or someone even more renowned. Why not? Who said that you can't? If someone watched me prepare for a concert, one might think that I was ready for the concert maybe three or four months prior to the concert day. In my mind, though, the piece is always marked as "not yet."

I believe something significant inside of us changes when we try to reach beyond the best version of ourselves. For me, it was never a competition with others, but pursuing the best without knowing where I was actually going. I do think that comparing ourselves with other people is toxic to our mind. As a result, to my surprise, and more often than not, I ended up being the one who stood out from the crowd, which I didn't intend as a goal. For instance, I ended up finishing one of the most rigorous doctorate programs in music from Indiana University in record time, and had a Carnegie Hall debut sold out without having any contacts in NYC.

But what's more important is that I have been able to reach beyond my personal best by giving it everything I've got. The level of proficiency I had achieved in the past became something I wanted to surpass. For example, I never thought I could be a top pianist in my high school, but I was. I never thought I could be playing at Carnegie Hall, but I did. I never thought I could receive so many messages about how my music affected audiences' lives positively, but I did. These results always seemed like miracles to me.

I hope that you don't put these observations into a simple conclusion, saying all of these things happened to me because I have something special like musical "talent." I honestly never thought and still don't think that I have something more special than others—like talent. If there is something there, that is the result of the real effort that I put into practicing. I endured the dark times and kept pushing past my limits, even when it seemed daunting. That's all. I could easily have stopped every time I faced a tough challenge and blamed it on my lack of talent or opportunity, believing that was the only limit to my success.

Instead, I put my trust in pushing forward. Every time I faced an obstacle, whether it was a new piece of music, a concert, or a personal challenge, I learned to blindly push forward with a sharp and conscious intensity, and I didn't stop when I felt it was "good enough." Because that's where the real change happens—when we reach what we think is our limit. I'm the only one who knows how intense my efforts need to be. As for what others see, it may look like I am pushing forward enough even when I don't, but I always know internally when I am pushing myself to my limit with all my efforts or am just aiming for "good enough." It always surprises me when I reach further than I thought I could. In some ways, I don't have any tangible expectation from my full efforts other than being conscious about them. I allow myself to be surprised by the outcome and to remain curious. As long as I give it my all, and work in the best way I know how to, I won't be left with any regrets.

You only know what the best is for yourself. No one can tell you when and what is enough. You honestly know what your max effort is. Once you do that, with all honesty, then a true sense of freedom will come to you. That, for me, is worth it.

I believe there is a right time for everyone to experiment with the winner's mindset, in whatever you are doing. Do you have an important presentation coming up? Do you have a new project you are working on? A new recipe? Try to commit yourself to doing the work in the best possible way. No self-negotiating to be just good enough—instead, aim to become the gold medalist in your world. Visualize that you are already the best in that field with the very thing that you are doing. Imagine you are someone like Picasso or someone else you admire in the work you are trying. Use them as an inspiration.

Imagine yourself doing an excellent job, but don't worry about the outcome you want—that is NOT your job. Your job is to stay humble and put in the hard work. Remember to enjoy pushing forward—I am very curious to know if this way of thinking will take you somewhere you didn't think possible. Might this open another door that you didn't expect? Could this break that invisible layer of yours for the first time? Lead to another discovery of yourself?

For me, this mindset gave me one of the most important qualities in my life:

Freedom.

By this I mean the ability to let go completely, without regrets. You are simply doing your duty, trusting in the process, and then letting the universe take you where you are made to go. You see, the universe cannot move you unless you move first; but once you do, a current will form beneath you and carry you somewhere exciting. It is totally up to you to make it happen. I promise you. Try it.

I am excited for you already.

SOMETHING TO TRY
WHENEVER YOU'RE READY:

- When was the last time you felt you made progress, big or small, toward becoming a better version of yourself? What did you do to make that happen?

- Do you believe your max efforts would make a difference in who you are, how you show up in the world, and who you become? When was the last time you consciously tried something really difficult? What was it? How long did you try?

- Let's try the following:

  » I want to make a full effort of doing _____.
  I do it for myself because it gives me joy to push something forward and feel I'm making progress in my life. I understand every change will always start from my point of limit. I am committed to doing this activity for at least *(duration)* _____. I don't expect any specific outcome from doing this, but it will give me joy and a sense of freedom, as I will not be left with any regrets.

4

REWRITE YOUR STORY

*I*t definitely felt like a failure. There was no gray area about it. I had simply failed to be admitted to Seoul National University in 1999, where I had always dreamed of going. It was the best and the most reputable university in South Korea. Being able to go to that university would have meant I'd been handed proof that I was worthy of a bright future in whatever major I chose. Instead, I got an acceptance letter from Busan National University in my hometown, Busan. I was discouraged that I would not be able to fly away from where I grew up and land in the bigger city, full of hope and possibility. As a silver lining, though, I received a full scholarship for the entire undergraduate study as the top student in the music department at Busan National University.

Honestly, I was also feeling somewhat relieved by the fact that I wouldn't have to go into debt to pay for my education. That day, I whispered to myself with slight disappointment, "Let's go to a bigger world than Seoul after this. Maybe I just need to jump into a bigger circle. Somewhere like America. I am just taking my time for my next flight, that is all." It was my way of coping with that situation without knowing what the future held.

Undergraduate time in Busan was rather uneventful. I lived at home and commuted to school from my own room in my mother's house, and there was not much excitement in the university environment either. It seemed like I was surrounded by the same people, the same familiar streets, and the same daily life with practicing piano. I endured the entire four years of my undergraduate education and felt like a bear going through a four-year-long hibernation with big dreams in my heart—dreams for something wonderful after Busan.

> I experienced this: I will fail. Many times. More than I wished. It is just a law of life, but I can always choose to learn tools about how to cope when I fall.

During those undergraduate years, I studied English in the hope of going to America soon after school. I went on a backpacking trip to Europe by myself for two months. I attended summer music festivals abroad whenever I could, and lived in South Carolina for a month as an exchange student. Then, when I finally got accepted into a master's degree program at Indiana University in the United States, I was more than ready to explore and face the challenge, whatever that would be. I jumped on a plane to America with a big smile on my face, although I cried hard at the airport when I said goodbye to my mom. It all felt like the right step to my new life opening up in a new country. I never looked back, nor have I since returned to live in Korea.

Looking back on the day I was rejected by Seoul National University, it all makes sense to me now. I understand the reason I did not enter that university then: It would have been too expensive; the new environment would have provided lots of distractions from the piano; and competition with so many other students may have led to burnout. Who knows, I may have lost my interest to go abroad and stayed in Korea. Whatever the reason, I realized that every piece of the puzzle made perfect sense in the overall picture of my life in those years.

Those four years of hibernation as an undergraduate in my hometown helped me spend the next fifteen years going through further stages of academic study with a doctorate degree and another master's degree afterward, guarding me from burnout as a pianist, which is the number-one reason for stopping piano among many musicians with similar backgrounds to mine. In fact, I only know about three out of one hundred pianists who'd been piano majors from my arts high school that same year as me who have continued playing piano after college. I'm sure they're content with their lives, even without continuing piano. I just can't help but wonder why they stopped. After all, they'd worked at piano for almost fifteen years of their lives. I wonder what would have happened if they'd kept going, despite the failures and setbacks, and how their lives would be different now.

> Rewrite your story in your head before understanding the big picture. You may never understand why certain failures occur, but you can choose to believe that it was a needed step for the next story of your life.

When I fail or receive discouraging news—rejection letters from jobs I've applied for, or for possible concert engagements, a divorce, a failed relationship with my own biological father with whom I don't keep in contact, the loss of a family member or beloved friend—the world seems always to fall down very hard and unexpectedly. I don't have to list all of my setbacks or dark periods here to remind you of how many failures we all go through in our lives—I know we all have a fair amount. But I've started to detect a pattern: The story of failure doesn't end there. It leads to something better. The very stumbling blocks that made me think my life was over ended up being crucial stepping-stones into the next stage of my life. All I needed to do was to endure my darkest winter, over and over again.

This is one thing I am sure of: I will fail.

Many times.

I will lose someone or something.

Over and over again. And it hurts. Often unbearably.

But there's something else that I've learned.

During my dark winter period, I need to rewrite the story in my head before it writes itself later in my life, and I do this by believing that it is the needed stone for another step. Simply remove the stigma in the story during the descent. I know, I know. It is so much easier to look back and say everything makes sense now, versus being in the middle of the storm and trying to stay positive. It does feel unnatural and almost inhuman to say, "Wow, this failure hurts so badly. It must be a really good one for my growth." No, I am not saying that you need to do that. But simply be aware of the fact that we all fail and enter low moments of our lives, which is just natural. Try to endure dark times with full respect for yourself, believing that it will get better.

Promise me this:
Don't make a decision out of fear, out of insecurity, out of disappointment, out of anger. When you are in the middle of low moments in life, simply do your daily thing. No blaming, no decision making. Just don't change anything. Do your normal work while you wait for the storm to pass.

When I say full respect for yourself during the low moments, it means you don't have to load yourself up with even more negative weight. Moving forward is hard. Change is hard. Falling and failing are so bitter and hurtful. When you are finally able to see the whole picture after you've come out of the hibernation mode—out of your dark winter—simply look back again and see objectively if there is any pattern—of choosing a bad relationship, of unproductive work, a lack of time, or maybe coping with depression in a less-than-healthy way. This may not be easy to determine by yourself, but as long as it looks like you can change this pattern and not end up making the same mistakes, it is ideal to accept what's happened and move on.

Sometimes, if there is a pattern that I notice I can change, then I simply try a new strategy. I warn you, though, try not to make any decision when you are weak or in hibernation mode—a time when you stay still and recharge. Wait for a while. Much longer than you would want to, sometimes. When you bleed, there are all sorts of sharks trying to get into your mind, making it very difficult for you to make wise choices. I find that hibernation time is healthy for all of us—no decision making, no blaming, just simply doing daily work and not changing the routine.

> Once you fully accept and try to understand that failures and hard times are truly blessings to your life, there is nothing to stop you from shining from the darkness. You are more special because of that.

When do you know you are over that hibernation period? For me, it's when I forget to notice how I am feeling down or bad, simply being able to feel good about sunshine in the afternoon, or the random scent of a wildflower on the street that makes me stop and smell it, and noticing that I feel content deep down. That spring day always comes when I least expect it. For me, some hibernations took years before I could get to the springtime of my life again.

What I wish for myself and for you is this: Try to consider the whole story in your head and rewrite your failure into one of the most beautiful pieces—even before you understand how that failure fits into the full picture. The positive mindset is sometimes not about thinking positively but accepting the failed or seemingly dark situation just as it is without putting yourself down—or giving up. Just believe that the day with good weather is waiting for you. You just need to walk through the storm.

 ## SOMETHING TO THINK ABOUT WHENEVER YOU'RE READY:

A suggested perspective to think about for yourself . . .

- I can clearly see now that the failure I had in the past (_____) was a great turning point of my life. It was a needed stepping-stone for my life.

- I accept that I will go through many difficult times and many failures in my life. I will feel bad and I will be hurt. That is normal.

- I accept that it takes time to get better—often longer than I wish. The good day is coming when I least expect it.

- I understand that moving forward is hard, change is hard, and failing is hard.

- I understand that continuing my daily routine regardless of my emotional difficulties is helping me mentally.

- I will not make any decision out of fear.

5

YOU CAN CONTROL
SOME THINGS,
JUST NOT EVERYTHING

*M*aybe it was the performance dress I was wearing, or the makeup that a friend put on my face for the special day, or maybe it was the piece I was playing. Whatever it was, during my teenage years, when I walked onto the stage for a live performance, it always felt to me like I was walking onto a bungee-jumping dock. I knew I was not going to die from it, but it really felt like I would come close—close enough that I'd need to shut my eyes hard in case I fell. Would I make it safely this time? Would the rope catch me?

There was no question that I have always loved piano. Live performances, however, often left me with a feeling of anticipating that something really bad would happen. When there were mistakes during a concert, I thought in my head, "There you go again," berating myself with a cynical tone.

I am not exactly sure when or how the shift happened in my feelings toward live performances. Probably it was slowly, and over many years. In fact, this book might give you some glimpse of my journey. Something definitely has changed in me over the last twenty years, since those days when I was in my early twenties. I no longer dread live performances. Do they make me feel uncomfortable? Yes. Those butterflies in my stomach just won't go away—but that doesn't mean it is all bad either. That's just the way it is. The difference now is that I am excited about a concert, even looking forward to it. The same girl who used to walk onstage as if preparing to go bungee jumping has now been replaced by a performer walking on a path with flower petals everywhere. I walk tall, with a big smile on my face for the audience, while they cheer back at me.

Elizabeth, one of my private piano students who was preparing to give a solo piano concert, was experiencing the same familiar discomfort with performances that I felt in my youth. She told me that she feared she would make huge mistakes and this would end very badly. Every time she came to a lesson, she told me that performing would be an awful idea not only for her but for the poor audiences who would have to listen to her. I thought that while this would not be a quick fix, I needed to trace myself back in time and recall how I found some solutions for myself to guide her to try. What *did* happen for me then?

> You view the world through your own lens. Remember to ask yourself if there is anything you should change in that lens.

Over the course of many live performances over many years, I've learned that people who come to a concert genuinely want the best for me and for themselves—they want to have a great experience. They are not there to pick up on all of the potential mistakes, like a jury panel, but are there for a shared, human experience. Okay, even if there is someone there to judge me, I still only have one way of viewing the world, and that is through my eyes. If I believe they are there to love my music, that IS the world that I choose to see. Whenever I go to a concert, I am already ninety percent there emotionally to be able to receive whatever the performer can give me, simply by making an effort to be there. I am open and ready to share the musical experience. Why would I ruin my next hour and my enjoyment of listening to beautiful music by being pessimistic and critical the whole time?

Most importantly, I choose to see my performances through the eyes of the most warm and loving audience member. My grandma, who passed away, never really understood or listened to classical music. I don't think she liked it. Her taste in music was more in line with traditional Korean pop music, called *Trote*. Despite her indifference toward classical music, whenever I played piano for her she looked at me with the most loving eyes and listened to

> Imagine the most loving and warmest person in the world, and assemble that person in your head. Then show your work to that person. Remember that feeling and turn around, always keeping that view as your own.

every note as if it might just fly away into the air and she needed to catch it. I'm sure she wanted to put her hands on my shoulder several times, as she often did, but when I played for her, she kept about a foot of distance from me and the piano, caressing my whole being simply with her existence. In her eyes, I could do no wrong. Even if I made a mistake, what would that mean to her? Absolutely nothing. I was already accepted—fully—without even playing a single note.

This is why, when I perform in front of any kind of audience, I think of my grandma, who was beyond ready to accept whatever it was that I created with music. To her, all was beautiful just the way it is.

See, it's a choice. I choose to see the world of performance through the lens of a compassionate person who would not judge me or compare me with others but would want the best for me. You get to choose whatever lens *you* want to see the world through. If you have a hard time changing that view, I encourage you to visualize it as vividly as possible. "Fake it until you make it" is an absolutely useful tool in my world. I visualize a concert coming up, as detailed as possible, with the exact scenario I would like to see played out. Even little silly details like when I will wake up, what I will eat, what I will wear, even what I will think—everything in the best possible scenario. When I visualize the final walk to the stage, I see the people cheering for me, with the most enthusiastic crowds, there to share this beautiful experience together. They are not thinking about the past or the future, nor are they comparing me to others. At that very moment of the concert, I am the only pianist in the whole world, creating music on this very piano at this exact moment of time for them. That unique experience takes place only once, right now, never again. I find that it is beautiful and liberating at the same time.

Not only do I visualize others to be warm listeners, but I also make sure I visualize myself to be an excited, generous, and loving pianist who is eager to share music with the world. I am not a pianist who would judge myself, I am not a pianist who would dread going onstage, and I am not a pianist who would compare myself with other pianists or only anticipate bad mishaps on the stage. I choose to be the precise type of pianist that I want to be in my head, well before I play a single note.

> Visualization is a powerful tool. You simply have to relive the best screenplay you already created in your mind in real life.

Who is that person you wish to be? What kind of people do YOU wish the audience to be? Unfortunately, the bad news here is that you can't change another person's view or thought. You only have control over your thoughts, your conscious intention of what you would like to see from others. That is different from asking others to act one way or another. Simply believe in your head that they are the people you wish them to be, and live your life as if they *are* that way. Their view is none of your business. Even if you hear harsh words from someone, let them be. They are just being whoever they are. You don't have control over them, but surely you do for your world. I would prefer a path with flower petals any day over a walk toward the end of a cliff.

Always ask yourself if you are hanging on to something that you cannot control. How wasteful and unproductive is that? Once you shift to doing something you can control instead, the positive flow will come back to you.

Often when we feel nervous or worried, we are thinking about something that we can't control. I attended a workshop about performance nerves when I attended an artist residency at the Banff Centre for Arts and Creativity. They asked musicians to divide a sheet of paper in two and write in the columns two lists: what we can control and what we can't control in life. I found this exercise very helpful in becoming more aware of my own mind. For example, we can't control time—the future or the past. We can't control random accidents that happen in life or even mistakes we make onstage, no more than we can shape others' preconceived opinions or preferences. And we can't always control what or how we feel. But we *can* control the way we think, our intentions, how we act in the present moment, how we prepare for an event, the way we talk to ourselves, and the way we view the world. When my student Elizabeth was nervous about her upcoming concert, she was so worried about other people's thoughts (which she can't control) that it led to her thinking she couldn't control how she would feel about the concert—ultimately, she was underestimating what she could actually control.

When you realize you are worrying about something that you simply have no control over, then just let it go and shift your focus to what you *can* actually control. If you would like a certain person to love your work, and they don't, there is nothing you can do to change that. But you can absolutely control how you prepare for it, what strategy you use, and how *you* view the work. There is always something you can do within the realm of what you can control. And making daily efforts to prepare for this is critical.

Choose to focus on what you CAN control.

Choose to let go of what you CAN'T control.

It's that simple. It may be that you just never realized it.

SOMETHING TO TRY WHENEVER YOU'RE READY:

- Make your own list of two columns: things you can control and things you can't control in life. This was a powerful exercise for me and helped me get this concept in my head more clearly. I highly recommend you try it also.

Things you CAN control in life	Things you CAN'T control in life
1. Ex) how to prepare for an event	1. Ex) mistakes/accidents

- Do you have a big presentation, concert, or event coming up? Try to visualize that important day in as much detail as possible—in the best-case scenario with the most positive version of yourself—and write that down. Imagine the best-case scenario playing out, detail by detail. Then, visualize it as often as possible before the big day.

6

STAY AWAY FROM THE MIND VIRUS

A new era has begun with COVID-19. As I write this during quarantine, I hear some people say that society will never be the same after this pandemic. The routines of washing hands around the clock and wearing a mask have become our new norms. A number-one tactic for everyone against this virus has been avoiding it, so we keep our distance from others and work on keeping our own immune system strong, in the event that we contract the virus.

But all this talk of COVID has gotten me thinking about the most dangerous virus that can infect our minds, and no amount of hand sanitizer can protect us from it. If there is a mind virus that works most viciously, it's the trap of self-pity. It may not be too contagious to others, but once it gets into our system it spreads quickly, especially when we feel weak or vulnerable.

When I first came to America to study for my master's degree, my mom promised

> We are the most susceptible to this self-pity virus when we mentally and physically feel weak.

me a year of financial support and told me that I needed to find a way to support myself after that. I said to myself, "Once I go to America, I will figure something out. A year will be enough time to do that." It turned out it was not as easy as I thought. I applied for a teaching assistant fellowship position right away, but I didn't get it that first year. Well, understandably. I was just fresh off the boat, so to speak. Everything was new—the language, the environment, and the culture. How could I expect anyone to hire a complete outsider to teach undergraduate students in the first semester—in a language still foreign to the teacher?

As the time approached when my financial support from Korea would end, my anxiety grew. I didn't want this lack of money to get in the way of my studies that I had waited four years to begin. I thought

> A new way of looking at the same situation with a different perspective has helped me realize that I have everything I need. I am alive.

that it would be unfair of the world to make me stop here and send me back to Korea, and just because of a simple lack of resources. At that point, as I recall, I caught my first mind virus of self-pity. I envied other students who could simply focus on their studies and practice piano as much as they wanted, entirely free from worrying over money. All I wanted was to study as much as I could. "Is that too much to ask?" I wailed to myself. "Why are there so many challenges in my life? How pitiful I am! I can't even practice long enough after my classes, as I need to make extra money!" The more I felt how unfair the situation was for me, the deeper I was swamped into the quicksand of this mind virus.

That was when I found out the news that a close friend of mine had been diagnosed with a brain tumor. When I met her for coffee, she said (with a smile) that she would probably be okay, that it wasn't fatal, but that after the surgery, there would be a great chance that she would not be able to move her hands or some parts of her body normally, the way she could now. She added that she was so relieved that the doctors had caught it so early, as otherwise surgery may not have been an option. She told me all of this as if it were another person's story, without asking for empathy from me, but rather in a neutral tone. I am sure all of this was really difficult for her to grasp. She was in her early thirties— surely too young to have to worry about this kind of thing! A sharp pain came into my heart, and I thought, "If I were in her shoes, would I be able to explain everything so calmly, without tumbling into the abyss of self-pity, or asking everyone I came across for some empathy?" I would most likely blame the whole universe for this. I would cry my eyes out, thinking how unlucky and forlorn I was, to get this tumor before doing anything with my life yet.

A change of perspective. That is what I experienced then.

Experiencing a crisis in life through my friend, I learned that the universe doesn't owe me anything. I am not entitled to receive anything more. I have already got the gift, called *life*. When I hear the age-old question "If you knew you were going to die tomorrow, what would you like to do today?" I always wish to say, "I want to do exactly the same things I did yesterday." That answer requires me to appreciate everything I do in my typical day: wake up in a comfy bed, enjoy the scent of mint tea in the morning and the sweet sunshine in the afternoon, play piano for hours, talk to a friend on the phone, read a book, do yoga, eat lunch. Even the mundane tasks I do all day, like washing the dishes, I want to do them too.

> Keep a neutral attitude as much as you can with a life challenge, without the companion of self-pity.

There is a lot of life advice out there along the lines of "Appreciate what you have! Write a gratitude journal! Be thankful!" Before just tuning it out as just another cliché, I want you to think about it for a moment. What are you grateful for *right now*? Just simply think of that thing for a little bit, hold that thought in the palm of your hand, and store it away inside of your heart.

I found that the real challenge to having this gratitude mindset is when you are going through challenges or dark moments. When you become the one who has a brain tumor, this mindset might be asking too much from yourself. I am not even sure how well I would do either. But I would try, as hard as I could, not to fall into the trap of self-pity. Maybe feeling gratitude might be too hard, but I believe we can simply accept the bad situation in a more neutral way, without a dramatic rendition of the poor-little-me saga. When I am going through a difficult situation, I might cry, and I might feel bad, but I try my hardest not to take the companion of self-pity along with me. Because as soon as that virus gets into our system, it eats up our soul, dragging us down into the deepest and darkest hole of depression. This is the real danger, as it is hard to dig out on our own—but at the same time, no one can help us dig out either. It's entirely up to us. No, the last thing I want to become is that poor monster who desires everyone to look at her with pity in their eyes.

> Think about one thing you're grateful for right now, and then put that into your heart and smile.

The easiest solution for avoiding this is to have a better immune system against this self-pity mind virus, and the first step is to become aware of its approach by using a frequent screening system. Just like checking my temperature for initial signs of COVID-19, I would check for this virus at any time that I'm feeling down or discouraged. As a side note, do not confuse self-pity with legitimate stages of grief or loss. We all need support and help from friends and family when we go through a loss and dark times, and we all require empathy when we are experiencing pain. I am talking here about a self-misery trap that you create in your head.

I understand that what you are going through right now could be the most miserable thing in the world. But, my dear warrior friend, in this war of life, let's try to fight back with the strongest armor we can find. I don't want you to feel any more suffering in this difficult war, or to hurt yourself. Ask for help from others without dragging yourself into the self-pity hole. Keep as calm as you can, and just as everyone advises, think about what you are grateful for today and at this very moment. Maybe you could write a list. Be creative with this list and include even the small and silly things. The feeling of a pen as you write, the supportive bed you slept in, a crispy apple you just bit into. The small or big things, and anything at all that brings you comfort and pleasure. Then savor that in your heart.

Having a screening system for the trap of self-pity as often as possible helps you catch it before it gets too big and makes you feel even worse.

Every time I stumble into this virus or begin dwelling consciously on the hope of not catching it, I practice this mindset every day over and over again. If anything, for me, I can catch it early, before it becomes dangerous.

Let's live today—the present—like it's a wonderful gift.

We've all received this gift.

It is called life.

SOMETHING TO TRY
WHENEVER YOU'RE READY:

- A self-screening test for the self-pity virus (choose yes or no):

  » I have felt that the current situation is unfair to me. (Yes/No)

  » I have felt that bad things are happening to me more than to others. (Yes/No)

  » People never understand my situation, as they can't experience it in my shoes. (Yes/No)

  » I don't want to do anything. I am miserable. (Yes/No)

  » I feel pity for myself. I have been going through a lot lately. (Yes/No)

  » More than 80 percent of what I told others and myself last week was related to how miserable I feel right now. (Yes/No)

  This list is here to help you be aware of your own thought process. This is not a criticism toward you. Only you can get out of this self-pity trap. Don't just sit and contemplate how bad your situation is and do nothing about it. Do something! Anything. Go for a walk. Let's start with that.

- Let's think about three things that you are grateful for today. Give at least one full breath in and out with each one to give enough time for this to sink in. Then smile.

What are you thankful for today or right now?

1. _____

   _____

   _____

2. _____

   _____

   _____

3. _____

   _____

   _____

지워받게.

INTERMEZZO OP. 118, NO. 2
BY JOHANNES BRAHMS

*B*rahms's Intermezzo Op. 118, No. 2 in A major is one of my favorite pieces of music. "Intermezzo" in general does not give us much information, other than it is an instrumental character piece that can stand on its own. Brahms's reputation and status as a composer are such that he is sometimes grouped as one of the "Three Bs" in classical music—Bach, Beethoven, and Brahms.

His early piano works often imitate the full sonority of an orchestra, with big chords that often require awkward hand positions that fit in many notes at once. Later in his compositions, which include this intermezzo, we can see he started to understand the piano as a much more intimate and delicate instrument, rather than squeezing an orchestra into one instrument. In this piece, it feels as though Brahms is composing only for piano, imagining only the sound of the piano.

When we see pictures of composers, it's hard to imagine their real character solely through their portraits. Brahms's portrait, the one we usually see, is the one where he is in his fifties, with a beard, a big belly, and a serious look on his face. However, when we encounter his younger portraits, which are much harder to find, we find a handsome man with ambition, sweetness, and great kindness in his eyes. I find that this intermezzo, despite his outer look of a serious and rather cold image, reveals an intimate and delicate soul—that of the picture from his youth.

The piece opens like a question to oneself, then settles into a gentle narration of a letter to a loved one. Something about this piece always breaks my heart to play and even to listen to. If I could have the ability, I wish I could go back in time and see what was taking place on that day of composition in Brahms's life. It always requires me to be completely vulnerable in order to express this heavenly piece of music as a pianist, without breaking into pieces while expressing it.

There are many letters and writings about his relationship with pianist Clara Schumann, who was the wife of another composer, as well as renowned music critic, Robert Schumann. When Brahms, in his twenties, knocked on the door of Robert Schumann's house, he was hoping to get a positive review from Schumann's magazine, *New Journal of Music*, and acknowledgment of his talent from Schumann for a promising career as a pianist and composer. That is how their intertwined relationship began, and they maintained a special connection throughout their lives. It is very well known that Brahms helped Clara a lot—especially when Schumann made multiple attempts at suicide and put himself into a mental hospital in his later life. Brahms was the person who stayed beside Clara to soothe her and be a great friend.[3]

I feel that this intermezzo is a love letter. Maybe it was for Clara, to whom this piece was officially dedicated, or perhaps it was for someone else. I see this music as a love letter that was never meant to be sent, almost as though the author wrote all of his emotions in a diary. I bet he never expressed his love to Clara, even after Schumann passed away. It is my opinion, however, that his sensitivity, heartbreak, sorrow, love,

---

3   If you want learn more about Brahms, check out the amazing biography by Jan Swafford, called *Johannes Brahms: A Biography.*

and passion have been captured in this form of music much more vividly than anyone could ever express in words.

I am curious to know if you can feel Brahms's emotion in this piece without knowing much about him as a person. Can you feel him? Can you feel his heartbreak? Can you feel the love? Let's enter the time machine together right now and receive that love letter.

Please go to my podcast, *Journey Through Classical Piano*, and locate Season 1, Episode 8. Close your eyes and listen to the Brahms Intermezzo Op. 118, No. 2. Please take your time as you embark on this trip.

To listen to the piece and learn more about it, scan here ▶

MOVEMENT #3

Create,
Dream, and Play

1

CREATE YOUR OWN PATH

*S*ometimes people still ask me, "So, what is your *real* job?" after I tell them I am a pianist. If they haven't heard my name before, they often assume I must have another more "legitimate" or "substantial" job to support my piano. Typically speaking, people know one way of becoming a well-known pianist—that is, by winning reputable competitions, such as Chopin or Van Cliburn or Queen Elizabeth. Winners will be given ample opportunity to get hooked up with a good agency, guaranteed concert engagements for the next three to five years, and sign contracts from major recording labels for albums during those years. Those competitions take place mostly for individuals starting around the age of eighteen and going up into the mid-twenties. After their late-twenties, there are a lot fewer competitions that a pianist can even enter.

These young musicians have to keep their competition repertoire up, like a tool they keep sharp for potential war at any moment. Competitions become their temporary job for at least three years, and sometimes up to ten. They keep showing up for any size competitions with mostly the same repertoire they have been practicing for years, hoping that the next time they try, they may advance further. However, the lottery tickets are limited, with an insanely miniscule probability of winning. Probably 0.00001 percent of musicians will win a major competition, after which they acquire the promise of opportunity and world recognition. Problem solved. But what happens to the other thousands and millions of pianists who attempted but failed in this competition pool? Problem not solved.

I always found that this competition strategy for a "real job" was too risky to get into. Too much luck is involved, and you need to be prepared to do this for at least three years, during a critical time of your life in which I also believe you should be learning something new and continuing to push forward in your education. The thing is, however, if you do become the one out of a million pianists who enter the major competition and win, this strategy

> We often think a certain job offers security. We need also to think what "security" holds. If you have the job and you are depressed about the work, is that secure?

does work. They are brave to risk a critical time of their lives, knowing they will deal with a hard mental battle if they lose. All you need is to win once—people will not remember the millions of times that you lost after you win a major competition.

Then there is another strategy for obtaining a "real job" in the field of classical music, and that is to keep pursuing a higher education. I don't think I chose this as a conscious strategy, but I fell into this category by default, since I didn't join the competition club. I ended up earning a master's and doctorate degree in piano performance from Indiana University, and then I was crazy enough to go back to school to get another education master's degree in piano pedagogy. While I enjoyed the pure joy of getting better at piano and my musical education, I didn't really think through what I was supposed to aim for professionally during those education years. Maybe I thought—unconsciously—once I finished all of the higher education, then those music agents would knock on my practice door to offer a contract to become a musician on their rosters or some schools would magically offer me a teaching job. I mean, that is what the world seems to ask you to possess as a default condition for those teaching positions or for potential concert credentials, a doctorate degree, right?

Instead, nothing happened after I got my degrees. Nobody came to my door to offer to record an album, nor there was any acceptance letter for a teaching position. Without questioning my true intention in seeking those real jobs, I pursued them anyway. I applied to many potential universities and inquired at potential agencies, spending countless hours writing emails and making phone calls. My main goal was simply to protect my love of piano from the world, so I could keep playing piano for the rest of my life. You know, I thought I needed to have a real job to support my *secret* real job—which is playing piano.

> When I closed one door completely, then and only then, a new door opened up to me. I am not sure if it always works that way, but for me, it was how the magic worked.

I am not sure why, but I went ahead and moved to San Diego before I received a solid confirmation of the promised lecture position at one of the area's universities. Until then, I was always affiliated with some university as an adjunct faculty to teach piano courses, while I performed concerts mostly in Chicago. I naively believed that this potential job offer was a done deal—until it wasn't. There were apparently some inner politics that led the powers-that-be to choose another person before I even got there. All of a sudden, I was left alone in a city where I knew nobody, and I was jobless and without connections. In this fairly desperate place, for the first time in my life, I questioned my job-hunting mindset.

"Why do I keep molding myself into a job description that the world defines?"

"What do I want to do? What am I good at?"

I realized that I was not actually excited about the university job itself, but only the bonus that comes with the position, such as a secure salary. Deep down, I knew I wanted to perform more, which was also contradictory to working as an academic. That is the moment that I decided to bet big. Not for the bonus, or salary, but just pursuing the job itself that I would love to do: playing piano, creating an album, and performing in concerts. That moment, I completely moved on from the idea of landing a position as a professor or whatever "real job" the world would have me do and decided to create my OWN real job.

I asked myself: What do I really like to do? I always liked teaching and forming a close relationship with students, seeing them grow into beautiful musicians themselves. I found it humbling, being a student together with my students. Teaching requires a different kind of creative process. The level of the students doesn't really matter to me, but the joy of helping them from point A to point B always excites me. I've noticed myself that I generally like to help people make sense of their world, whether that comes in the form of playing a certain kind of music, how to listen to music, how to practice more efficiently and successfully, how to cope with performance nerves, or even how to create a positive lifelong habit. It all feels like a big fun life puzzle to me, and I like to solve it together with others.

> You know yourself better than anyone does. What are you best at? Create your own dream job in your head based on your strengths. Forget the world for now and have fun with your imagination.

Then I really do love performing. In my mind, my first identity is being a pianist, who happens to love to teach also—not the other way around. From the stage as a pianist, I applied this educator's lens with my choice of repertoire and how to approach the concert. I wanted a concert to be a shared experience, not a passive participation. I certainly didn't want to be that pianist who performs on a stage then disappears backstage. That is where the idea for my first album and concert project, *10 More Minutes*, began in my head. After much trial and error with performing and teaching in various settings up to that point of my life, I finally arrived at the discovery of what I could offer to the world with my unique background and my own personality, combined with my passion for piano and my educator's mind. My goal was to change the concept of a classical piano concert into something that was approachable and friendly for anybody who was interested.

Just like a strategy for entering competitions, or another strategy of writing numerous job applications for a teaching position in higher education, this time I created my own third strategy approach, which was putting out this album and concert idea, *10 More Minutes*, to the world through a Kickstarter crowdfunding $30,000 pledge.

To make a long story short, yes, it was successful. At first it was my idea, and then it became everyone's project, with their active participation in supporting it. My base of fans grew, as people who believed in my dedication as a pianist started to follow my concerts. People loved the connection I created for them to better understand classical music concerts. Some fans have called me the "gateway drug" to classical music. My Carnegie Hall debut concert with *10 More Minutes* was a sold-out event with people who came from out of state to hear me again after listening to this concert other times in their area. This unreal dream, like the first step into my *real job*, simply started with the decision to stop trying to fit myself into society's box.

I have to say that it was not an easy decision to ditch the university option completely. After all, I am qualified and trained well to teach in higher education, and I did like the thought of having the security and respectability provided by university jobs, even though such a career wouldn't support my primary identity as a performer. In many ways, after having so many university doors closed on me, I was pretty much forced to create my own track. But at the same time, I know I can continue to apply for a university position even now, teaching one or two courses as a lecturer with the hope of working my way up to a tenured position. It's never too late to reset your intention and start to think in a new direction.

But I do believe we often need to close one door before we can open a new one. In my case, once I said no to pursuing teaching jobs in higher education, a new possibility entered my life. It felt like an invitation: to play piano as I wish, start my own projects, and teach piano on my own terms. What was interesting was that once I left the notion of getting a fixed job position, I could see clearly that working in academia would not fit me. I would have disliked the not-so-fun aspects of working at universities, such as writing numerous emails, being obliged to sit through long meetings, teaching the same basic courses that often non-enthusiastic students are taking only to get requisite credits. It became clear to me that such work could become a slippery slope toward feeling depressed, despite the sugarcoating of financial security.

> Sometimes advice that you receive might not be so helpful. Think for yourself, listen to your gut feelings.

I wondered to myself, "Would that really make me feel *secure*?"

Once I abandoned this idea completely and created an objective space between me and what I was chasing, the answer was clearer than ever. I wanted to create a job where I could happily accept the negatives that come with it. Yes, working for myself does come with its own difficulties, but for me it mattered much more that I needed to love the work itself. I wasn't looking forward to a scenario where I would be waiting for the day to come to an end, watching the clock ticking.

What I do on a daily basis is the exact thing I enjoy doing most. My day is filled with what I choose to do. There will always be someone who advises us to pursue a career within a certain field just because it is *real* in their world. What I figured out was that we all are unique in our own way, and only I can create the best niche for me, in a way that highlights my strengths. No one knows better than I what's best for me. When I kept pushing in this direction with this mindset, the money that I needed eventually and inevitably just followed. Problem solved.

The most difficult part was to do this not halfway, but all the way. I am not sure if this is needed for everyone, but for me, this was a magic solution. Once I devoted myself to something that I knew was the best for my strengths, it eventually worked. You may prefer to choose a traditional track, and that's totally fine. A traditional job might be the best for you, based on your personality and strengths. However, if you feel that you are not

> Be your own boss. That is an experience that I wish for everyone to have at least once.

suited to a fixed job or you keep hearing "no" from the job search, maybe there is another possibility—perhaps there's a new path waiting for you.

With COVID-19, we've all been forced to change the way we work and the way we see what used to be secure job positions. We may need to find ways to deliver the core values of what we do without physical contact, even after this crisis is over. Many jobs have disappeared, and new ones have been and are being created. We may be forced to create something new. As much as it can be daunting and frustrating, it can also be liberating to reset one's life course. The change is already here, we just have to be much more active and forward thinking to accept it.

What are you good at? What would you like to do so much that you could endure any difficulties that come with it? If you could create your own dream job in this new digital world, what would that be? It may not exist yet in the world. Have fun with it. Imagine that dream job. Is that really just a dream? What would be the first step into that dream job? If this were a real-life fantasy video game that you were playing, what would you make the character work toward? Is there any skill set or education you can acquire now, to get closer to that dream position?

With the changes created during the pandemic, I began thinking about opening up more possibilities of livestreaming concerts for global audiences in a local concert hall, creating online piano courses to teach students around the world, and a new way of creating an album with a flash drive instead of CDs. Even with ongoing changes, I am doing exactly what I like to do—performing and teaching piano, talking about piano, and being my own boss. That is my dream job. I am CEO of the Jeeyoon company that I created for myself. I am not counting the days until I retire, or watching the clock until I am done with work. No one has to tell me what to do. I decide.

All I can say is that if I can do it, you can do it too. It is very liberating to be your own boss. I highly recommend it.

 SOMETHING TO THINK ABOUT WHENEVER YOU'RE READY:

- Think about your current job. Do you like what you do or simply like the paycheck? What are the aspects that you like and dislike about your current job?

- How could you adapt your current work to the new world we are facing with the COVID-19 pandemic? Is there anything you find that is more effective with our new digital world? How can you keep your core offering to the world without physical contact?

- Are you retired? Even better! You have a total white canvas to begin fresh on. How exciting! If you could create something you would love to do for the rest of your life to keep engaged and involved, what would that be? What makes you happy? What can you do well to solve the problems of others? Do that and create ways to share with others.

- Are you still searching for your job, but getting nowhere? What aspect of the job you are searching for is so appealing to you? The work? Or financial security?

- Have you thought about creating your own job?

  » This kind of thinking requires you to be an entrepreneur, but don't think about money yet, just think about *what problem you can solve for people* in your own way.

    ◊ I can _____ for people.

  » Let's create a new dream job based on your criteria. Have fun with it. Don't limit this job just because it doesn't exist yet in the world.

  » What is something you can do about it right away? You can simply research more about it on the internet, or write about this thought in your diary, or find books about the subject. Anything, small or big, just do it. Now.

2

REDEFINE YOUR SUCCESS

*G*etting a tenured position at a university would have been my mom's dream of success for me. Then my grandmother used to tell me that marrying a rich husband and becoming a professional housewife, playing piano every now and then, would have been a great success. I am sorry, Mom and Granny. I did not succeed at either of those, nor wished them as my own success.

After a big concert, especially one hosted at a prominent venue like Carnegie Hall in New York or the Conrad Prebys Performing Arts Center in La Jolla, California, there is always someone who tells me that one day in the future, I will be successful beyond my wildest dreams. Then the next person says I must be so happy being such a success. It's one or the other for these people: I'm either on my way to success, or I've already achieved it. These assumptions make me uncomfortable, but I let people imagine whatever they like. It is their story, not mine.

Everyone has a different view of that perfect picture of success, yet often it seems to come down to numbers. If you have X amount of money, then you are successful. If you win a major competition, then you are successful. If you have X number of followers on your social media, then you are successful. If you sell X copies of your album, then that album is noteworthy. Then, of course, once you reach those successful numbers, you will need even more to keep feeding that feeling of being successful. It's an upward climb with no ceiling.

I find that this picture of success is often elusive. We never have enough of it. The goal becomes a moving target. If you have X amount, then you want more on top of that. If you win a competition once, then you need to achieve other recognition from another place. Once you reach a goal, you need to go further. We rarely hear the full stories behind many of the obvious successes, either. Why would one of the most successful actresses commit suicide? Why has the winner of the most recognizable piano competition never performed in public again, due to depression?

> **What would it be like to describe "success" without any numbers? Dollars, friends, social media followers. What story would you tell?**

Once, I performed in a monastery in Chicago, where monks meditated and spent their training in a small and humble environment. I loved the experience of performing there in the peaceful environment of the temple. No, it was not with a Steinway concert grand piano, but it was a well-tuned upright piano tucked away in a corner. It was rather an unusual place to be filled with classical piano music, yet about fifteen monks that night were most enthusiastic and happy. That must have been one of the most special experiences I've had as a pianist. After that concert, when I listed that venue in my bio, one of the presenters in my next concert suggested I leave that place out, as it was not noteworthy enough to a general audience and it didn't show big ticket sales. Although I nodded with an understanding of these standards, I could not help but feel an ache in my heart. I wondered, "What is success? What does a successful life look like to *me*?"

In music, even though we do our best to numerically organize one pianist and the other, one concert and the other, such as, so-and-so is the third-place winner of the one competition, or so-and-so is number one in Beethoven sonatas inter-pretation, we can't really define a musical experience in any order. Its quality and success is a mere opinion of people, but that doesn't mean that one perfor-mance is not as beautiful as

> Ask this question often: "What does a successful life look like to me? What makes me happy?" No one can define that for you.

another, or we can't be deeply touched by it if one performer isn't as highly ranked as another. In fact, I am often touched by even a young child's performance, the way they perform with such beauty and sin-cerity. Where are they in this success system? Number 100,493?

To the typical media interview question of "What is your next goal for success?" I always answer somewhat vaguely. "To keep doing what I am doing with the piano," I say. The thing is, if you look at me from an outside point of view, I may look like someone who keeps chasing something for success. I create one album after another. I am a podcaster, YouTuber, writer, teacher, public speaker, and, most importantly, concert pianist. I tackle all of these with intensity, yet for me it is merely a fun game of a life with the goal of creating music

---

Play the game of life with joy, playing it hard yet not putting a value on the outcome. Ask yourself, "Did I enjoy it? Did I help some people? Did I have fun in the process?" Isn't that successful?

---

and connection. I may get some results or I may not. I have no control over the outcome. What's important to me is maintaining balance in this mindset: going at it with full intensity, yet not attaching self-value or a specific meaning of success. What matters is that I created something out of joy, that I touched some people in a meaningful way, and I had fun in the process.

At the beginning of my YouTube journey, I often found myself checking how many new followers had subscribed to my channel or how many new likes there were. I checked multiple times a day, as if the number was the only proof of the worth of what I created. Even though there were always some sincere comments about how much viewers enjoyed or how much they valued the video, I found it hard to stop caring about those numbers—in part because I had put so much effort into creating those videos. Who wouldn't want others to value something you cared about and put out to share with the world? Yet I learned that the world often doesn't care. They may never care at all about what you do. Accepting this fact without any anger or frustration is a must, a critical mindset, in this game. However, I learned that there is always, always someone out there who values your work. May not be thousands, but surely one feels invested.

> The world often doesn't care about what you do. Accepting this without anger or frustration will help you move forward on your own journey.

For me, my dream of success does not depend on what I do, but on the status of my being. I do what I love to do with my life on a daily basis. My picture of success precludes that my inner self would not be shaken by not only my own negative voice, but also any outside failures. I want to keep my mind content, simple, calm, and able to generate a self-energized feeling of accomplishment with what I create and love doing. That is true success in my world. It feels as though the target always moves, though, as one day I feel I get close, and other days not so much. But I keep trying to chase it anyway.

Yes, I do keep pushing my limits, having dreams of places I would like to perform, music that I would like to learn, projects that I would like to create, new things and places that I would like to explore, and more financial freedom. It would be meaningful for me also if I could reach an even wider audience with my music, and if my music gave people inspiration, joy, peace, and whatever else would make them feel good about themselves and the world from listening to it. While these are my goals, I don't feel I'm unsuccessful until I reach them. In my heart, I feel that I am already successful if I am content *now*, and I am not being mentally and emotionally affected by outside factors. When a storm arrives, I would like to be able to keep my attention and focus in a calm manner.

Am I successful today? Will I be successful tomorrow?

More often than not, nowadays I am fairly successful, by which I mean I am peaceful and happy, creating joy with my music. This may be difficult on some days, but that is my goal: not to be shaken by anything, keeping my center peace in place. When I stopped chasing for the things that the world worships, the real success for me knocked on my door.

What is your picture of success? At the end of the day, I just want you to be happy. That is all. I hope you are not limiting yourself to being happy "only if" you accomplish something tangible or expected of you. I bet you can be happy and successful today, right now, if you choose to. The answer might not be on the outside. Try to find it on the inside.

SOMETHING TO THINK ABOUT
WHENEVER YOU'RE READY:

- Trace back to the last time that you felt perfectly content. What were you doing? What were you thinking? What made you feel that way?

- Let's try to envision an image of success as the status of your being—as content, calm, and peaceful. What brings you close to that feeling?

    1. I am content when I do/think about

       _____.

    2. I am calm when I do/think about

       _____.

    3. I am peaceful when I do/think about

       _____.

Let's repeat those activities each day. Don't wait for success. You are successful *now*.

3

WHAT YOU DO MATTERS

*E*verything we do has its own dark side. If you are a surgeon, you save people's lives, but you may have to work crazy long hours, sacrificing personal time with your family and yourself. The fate of people's lives is in your hands, creating a stressful environment. If you are a ballet dancer, you express yourself with an art of movement and body, but you might suffer from many injuries and may always have to watch what you eat.

Being a pianist, I get to share the beauty of music and connect with people on a deep level, but I have to practice daily, for countless hours, and maintain that discipline for a lifetime. The longest I have ever gone without playing a piano was about a week. Even when I go on vacation, the first thing I secure before even booking my hotel room is a practice space. The last time I visited Korea for a holiday, my mom asked me, when I was about to leave for my practice at a local studio, "Isn't it okay not to practice sometimes if you have practiced for thirty-seven years?" I didn't respond but simply smiled back. I know. I sometimes wonder that too. *That* is perhaps the part that I sacrifice being a pianist. (If that is a sacrifice at all.) The focus of my whole being has always started with the notion of practicing piano. That means I have to say no to many things that people typically might do on many occasions, including simple social outings.

> Nothing we do is simple and easy. When we love something very much, we endure challenges that come with the work.

It would be a lie to say this has never been difficult for me. As much as I love what I do, on some days, I just want to forget that I am a pianist and take a long break from those shiny black and white keys. I have even fantasized about going on a trip for a whole year without worrying over practicing the piano. Then that thought frightened me—as I imagined life without the piano. I have learned to set that whining voice aside and just sit down and practice.

Many of my friends who majored in piano at university but have since given up the instrument often comment to me, saying, "I don't know how you do it. It always seemed to me that I had to choose between the two, a person with a normal life or being a pianist. Both don't seem to go together."

The reality is, sticking with the piano has *also* been a challenge for me. It's never been easy. No matter how long I have been doing this, being a pianist challenges me in every way almost daily. I choose it though. Why? Let me tell you my secret.

Often, I think about why I play the piano and my bigger mission as a person and a pianist. Just like a company has a mission statement, I think about my own mission frequently. Of course, it is not anything grand, like saving the world or fixing one of its many challenges, but I really believe that we all are here on this earth to do something good, big or small. Maybe some days, just a small act of kindness such as smiling at a stranger or picking up trash on the street will have a positive effect on that day, which may result in some butterfly effect in another way. Everyone has the unique opportunity to do something useful and beneficial each day.

Over the years, I've learned that playing piano is a magical power that I'm able to use to help people in a positive way. I can introduce this magical power in music to someone who may not get it otherwise. I want to be a sort of missionary for classical music. It is not just a means of making a living for me, but an ability to help others transcend mundane daily realities and help them heal and find joy in music. I happen to play the piano; thus, I have that unique ability.

> We are here on earth for a reason. It is our duty to do something good and look for the mission that is uniquely designed only for you to do.

That to me is my mission, to offer a connection between music and people so that the magical possibility in music is available to everyone. I strive to do that by incorporating the concept into everything I do—teaching, performing, creating albums, talking, and perhaps even this very writing.

I always thought it would be like neglecting my responsibility for doing good if I just stopped playing piano due to challenges that I faced. After all, I have been playing piano since I was four, and I never questioned that I would not be a musician. Whenever I was tempted to move away from the piano or whenever there were obstacles in life, my mission statement held me together. I strive to be a person who delivers the power of music to the world, helping people be inspired and connected and discover their own beauty and the beauty of the earth.

At the end of my life, I want to say that I know I have made good use of the path that was set before me. I can't just give up or not do it because it's difficult. Achieving anything that has true meaning and purpose is difficult in life, but I know we each have a unique duty to fulfill as we contribute to the world. It is not about saving the world in a big way, but one concert at a time, one person at a time, one day at a time, one note at a time. I need to be aware of that mission of doing good for the world with whatever I can do at every moment of each day.

Having a mission beyond just fulfilling my own life's need or self-satisfaction was one of the key incentives for me to keep going despite difficulties and failures. I am one of those important pieces in the puzzle of the universe—we all are! We each have a reason for being here. It could be to teach English in a school, or build a house, or cook, or create software, or it could even be something as small as talking to a friend who is having a hard time with a recent challenge, or helping someone you don't even know. We always need to keep looking for that reason and asking ourselves if we are on the right track. The small voice inside will always tell you, if you listen. For me, this process helped me look at my life more objectively and more positively, and in turn that helped me overcome discouragement and failure.

> You never know the butterfly effect on your goodness or your intention of helping others. Maybe that was your mission for that very moment. Always pay it forward. It is actually coming back to you bigger.

What can you do to help people? How can you help? Small or big, that is the first step when you form your mission statement. I don't think, without my mission statements, I could keep up with everything I do as a pianist or as a teacher or even as a person. My intention is to help someone with what I do. Whether I can is not as important as simply putting my intention in the right place, from the right place in my heart. *That* is my job, not the result itself.

The secret of life?

Look for your own unique mission in life. Remove yourself from that picture and perform your duty to make this great puzzle of a universe better. I bet you will be much happier and fulfilled to know that you made a difference. Just remember, there is no one like you in this world. Only you can do what you're here to do—and do it in your own unique way.

SOMETHING TO THINK ABOUT WHENEVER YOU'RE READY:

- Imagine yourself as a big company. When I go to your imaginary website for this company, I would like to see your mission statement. Can you form a few sentences that resonate with you about the person that you want to be, principles that you believe in, and the things you want to do in your own way?

  » I believe in _____. I can always help someone in this world with my own unique skills or my character by doing _____. I always strive to _____.

- Your way of finding a mission in life should reflect who you are and what you excel at. If you fix houses as a handyman, you are contributing to the world with your interests and strengths by helping people solve problems with their homes. If you are a full-time mother, you are impacting your child's life in the most significant way, more than anyone in this world can. Your impact will create a butterfly effect on other people, now and in the future. Every small thing you do influences everyone around you. You are the influencer of the universe.

- Do a random act of kindness whenever you see a chance. It can be as small as holding a door for a person behind you. Always look for an opportunity to help. Imagine the good butterfly effect to that person and the world by your small act. The world may not always recognize or appreciate your efforts, but keep doing your piece of the puzzle for the universe.

4

INDULGE YOUR DREAMS

I was holding a postcard of Carnegie Hall with a handwritten note for me by the eminent pianist Mitsuko Uchida. It said, "Why NOT?" Apparently, a friend of mine who attended Uchida's recent concert at Carnegie Hall had asked her to write that note for me. Over the years, people often asked me when I would perform at Carnegie Hall. Playing at Carnegie Hall sounded wonderful, but I never thought about it as being possible or, to be honest with you, necessary.

In many ways, I did not hold that as my dream until I received that message. As I held that postcard with a note from the pianist I admired, something inside me lit up with an idea: It would be wonderful to play there. It would be amazing to share my music with the world's landmark concert hall, in the heart of New York City. Dreaming this dream was fun, imagining walking into a beautiful hall with chandeliers, amazing acoustics, and a full audience. I could see myself playing one of the best nine-foot pianos, sharing this once-in-a-lifetime kind of experience with everyone in the audience. It would be an amazing concert. I could feel it!

Next morning, you know what I did? I called Carnegie Hall. Yes, that is correct. *I* called the booking office of Carnegie Hall. That itself was very courageous, I thought. (Or borderline crazy.) Before even ringing the second time, a lady picked up the phone.

"Carnegie Hall, booking office."

I had to hold my breath for a second, as I didn't expect anyone to answer the phone so quickly.

"Hi, umm, I am a classical pianist, Jeeyoon Kim. I am just calling today to ask something. This may sound funny, but . . . my question is what does it take to perform there?"

As I spoke, I was fully aware of how ridiculous I might sound, and at the same time I was wondering how many times she got this kind of call from all over the world. Luckily, she did not chuckle or sound puzzled—she simply gave me the steps that I would need to take and did so in a very businesslike manner. No, her answer was not "Practice, practice, practice," like the punch line to the old joke.[4]

> Dreaming is a muscle.
> Ask yourself, "Why not?"

Rather, the answer was about the importance of having the right presenter who could present my concert there and submitting the form that they needed to verify my credentials. After hanging up, I felt a weird yet empowering sensation. It was sort of like I was stepping into a movie that I was watching in real life. In that exact moment, playing at Carnegie Hall was not a dream anymore, but simply something I needed to follow through on to make happen over time. I had taken my first step into my dream.

I called possible potential presenters who had presented me in the past to discuss the option, and I finally found a good match: Jim Fung, from Captivate Artists in the San Francisco Bay Area. He had always

---

4   For those of you who may be new to the joke: A pedestrian on 57th Street sees a musician getting out of a cab and asks, "How do you get to Carnegie Hall?" Without pause, the artist replies wearily, "Practice, Practice, Practice."

been a big fan of my music and had recently presented me in that area. After our initial phone call, he was surprised yet also excited about the idea. Over time, we finally made a deal with steady and clear steps.

So, there it was: my Carnegie Hall debut, set for December 14, 2017. It was a sold-out concert, with many people hailing from all over the United States. The space was alive with enthusiasm and excitement. When I walked out onto the stage, the first thing I said to the audience was "Welcome to my dream."

I found that, even often for myself, it is hard to dream. We often put ourselves into a reality box, and don't let our crazy, wild ideas out to walk around. Just like our physical muscles, the less we use our dreaming muscle, the harder it becomes, as that part of us weakens over time. I asked my students in my group piano class what were their dreams regarding piano—the wildest, craziest dreams they could think of. They all looked almost paralyzed—stuck in their own boxes, unable to come up with anything. Their dreaming muscle was weak. Even if they wanted to keep their crazy thoughts to themselves, they acted like they could not dream. When I finally asked them to scale down that dream to something much smaller, only then were they able to breathe naturally again, answering something like their wish to play a piece like Chopin Ballade No. 1, or give their own recital having memorized all the pieces, and so on. They also revealed that they actually don't have crazy and wild dreams about anything. This led me to wonder:

Do we need to dream, then? If so, why?

I often think that to dream requires a certain muscle in our mind. We often put ourselves in a box and tell ourselves we're allowed to play only inside that box—a place where everything is visible and predictable. When we try to reach beyond those limits, often the judging,

> When I acted on the first step into a dream, the dream became no longer a dream, but a project with steps.

rational mind and our own limited worldview work actively against it, censoring our freethinking side. It is as if there would always be someone (who is most likely yourself) ridiculing the idea—the dream outside that box—as soon as you think of it. Seriously, what is wrong with dreaming, being open to a new possibility, a new crazy thought that may not seem possible now?

Why not?

We have limited vision. It is impossible to predict our future. We never know what the future holds, what kind of opportunity may come along, what kind of people we will meet, or what kind of life events will affect who we are becoming. I believe that dreaming, even in the vaguest form, plants a seed in our head, which can grow in a direction that we might move toward in the greater scheme of life. Honestly, if I hadn't dreamed of playing at Carnegie Hall, I don't think I ever would have played there.

There is another important fact here that I would like to emphasize. That is the fact that I called Carnegie Hall. I just picked up the phone and called. That first step made a huge impact on that dream becoming a reality. There were only two things I needed to do: dream and take the possible first step toward that.[5] If I am ready, the dream will catch me in the right time. If dreaming is planting a maple seed, adding water is the first step. Often there will be many long periods of time spent waiting and simply working without much progress, but without the seed planted and the first step of adding water, we will never grow a tree.

> Dreaming points you in the direction you want to go. The first step allows you to move toward that direction.

I often find that dreaming and having a learner's mindset go hand in hand. When you are comfortable being a total beginner in a field

---

5   Okay, there is a third thing, which we have covered already: practice!

you don't know, that willingness to be vulnerable helps you be open to new possibilities. It is an almost contradictory feeling, of being so vulnerable in the field that you are learning that you are made to be more open to dreaming. I find that avid learners are often some of the happiest people I've met. If you are learning something you are interested in, that means you are putting in the work, you're engaged, and you understand that effort and discipline will bring you joy with each breakthrough you have. You are also dis-

> Learners are one of the happiest and most positive groups of people I've met.

covering something about yourself outside the box. That doesn't mean all learners become instant dreamers, but a mind open to learning helps us be open to a new possibility, and eager to explore more.

Are you learning something? Are you dreaming? If you could dream wild in terms of something you create, or your work or your hobby, what would that dream look like? Remember, this is just a game and a muscle building exercise in our mind. It is really fun to create a huge circle around yourself and allow yourself to play without that close boundary we erect for ourselves. Indulge your dreams and keep questioning your true potential, and think about one small step you can take toward that wild dream today. Just remember, I called Carnegie Hall. No one knocked on my door.

Be a crazy dreamer. I will stick with you—smiling the whole time.

SOMETHING TO THINK ABOUT WHENEVER YOU'RE READY:

- Close your eyes and try to dream the wildest and craziest dream.

- Then ask that dream, "Why not?"

- If that dream represents a direction you would like to go, what is the tiniest and smallest action you can take today?

- Don't be discouraged if your wild dream is not achieved in the near future. It is still great to dream, to let yourself loose and head in a new direction. You can always slow down or even pause in life. The speed is not important, but having a sense of direction is.

5

SHARE YOURSELF

*A*s I was driven from O'Hare Airport into downtown Chicago, I started to have a small talk with my Uber driver, who looked to be in her forties. "Do you like to go to classical music concerts?" I asked. She answered in a short sentence: "No." Without giving up hope, I told her that I was a classical pianist and shared a brief, enthusiastic description of my upcoming concert in town that weekend. I said, "You might like this concert. I would love to have you come. Here are two tickets if you change your mind."

The Uber driver indeed showed up at my concert that weekend, approaching me after the concert. It took some time for me to recognize who she was. She said, "It was my first classical concert ever! And I loved it! Thank you for your invitation."

I smiled broadly. "I am so glad to hear that." I felt good that I made yet another conscious effort to share and connect. This act of promoting my concerts and sharing my work with a stranger runs totally counter to my natural inclination and tendencies. It is extra difficult when a person says no or seems indifferent. But I still put a smile on my face and talk about it, as I have learned that it is also a part of what I do, as much as playing piano is. There is no one better than myself to describe my upcoming concert, no one better to represent myself, sharing my passion.

With my piano students, we always have a piano recital at least three times a year. Initially, they mostly dread these recitals and try to avoid sharing news of them with others. Then, what they all end up seeing is that they learned the most by sharing a piece of music that seemed complete to them by having others listening. In the act of sharing, their understanding of the particular piece of music deepens, and a light shines within them. People say that if you want to learn something, try to teach it to others. Something within us seems eager to share with others. I find that it is our nature to want to feel as though we belong and contribute to society. No matter how many times I play a piece of music in my practice room, as soon as there is another human being listening to my music, it finally becomes something alive. It becomes a new identity that lives within me and them. The connection we achieve through sharing—whatever that may be, your work or passion or both—is truly special and helps you deepen your relationship with it.

> Share what you do with others. Something within you will light up by doing it.

In my university years, there were always degree recitals by fellow piano majors each semester. What was interesting to see was that there were definitely two groups. The first group of pianists absolutely wanted you to be there, inviting everyone they knew, putting posters around campus, talking about it excitedly to anyone they met. The second group didn't want you to be there. Well, I am not sure if that is totally true. Maybe they wanted you to be there, but they did not put any effort into inviting people. If you happened to talk about it, they would say, "Oh, well, sure, come by if you like. But not a big deal. Don't sweat it if you can't make it." They definitely didn't present it as a party that you didn't want to miss. They always seemed shy or uncomfortable talking about it. They had put so much work into playing those repertoires, yet they neglected and perhaps disliked the part of inviting people to the concert.

In fact, the level of performance had nothing to do with this attitude. Those performances with just a handful of audience members were often fabulous, and it almost felt illegal not to be able to share them with more people.

If I hadn't trained myself to make a conscious effort to share what I do, it would actually feel much easier for me not to mention anything about it. I think it comes from my Asian upbringing, where I learned that not bothering people too much is a virtue. Self-PR was taught as a behavior to avoid when I was young in South Korea. What I learned over the years, however, is that you need to be your own best agent first. Unless you advocate for what you do, people may never understand or care about what you do. Why would people be interested in what you do when you are not even enthusiastic about it? As

Let the world join in your playground. Let us glimpse into your passion. Not only the final work, but also the process of your work—sweaty, not finished, not polished.

a musician, I might put the work of promotion in the hands of another person, an actual agent or PR person, or a concert presenter. However, I have learned that the more I share about my project, with my own enthusiasm backing that sharing, the more people get to know me and engage with me, and the more they understand the essence of the project. Enthusiasm is always contagious. The less I talk about it, the fewer people find a connection with what I do.

When I decided to create my own career path, I formed my own agent company too, called Namus Classics. I am the owner and the sole performer in this agency, and I was the only one who worked for this company for a while. When I attend big performing arts conferences such as APAP (Association of Performing Arts Professionals) in New York City, there are literally thousands of presenters and agencies from around the world, all gathered to network. I put up posters and banners in my booth in the exhibit hall by myself, and I stand there for hours waiting for the presenters to come by. When I first attended the performing arts conference, I was overwhelmed by the pressure to talk about what I do, much like a salesperson would, and having to meet thousands of unfamiliar people in the industry for the first time. There are very few solo musicians who represent themselves in this way. I often felt insignificant next to big-name agencies like IMG or Columbia. Every morning, when I left the hotel room, I had to give myself a big pep talk. "Jeeyoon," I would tell myself, "you are doing great. You have lots to offer to the world. I know it's difficult to meet new people in this kind of setting, and mostly you will hear no or only indifferent responses today. But remember, this is just a process so you can get to an audience to share your music as the pianist that you are. So, for today, be your best agent."

> Your enthusiasm for what you do is contagious. Sharing will impact the world around you positively, and then come back to you with an even bigger impact.

I don't recommend everyone become their own agent professionally. In fact, I am starting to delegate that part to others more and more in order to focus on music making. But I learned so much by practicing this concept and stepping into the unknown territory surrounding it. Even if you are not literally your own agent professionally, you are still your own agent for what you do—your hobby, your project, who you are, and your work.

This feeling of not wanting to share is often rooted in our fear of judgment, or a perfectionist mindset: Unless it is perfect, it is not worthy of sharing, and we should wait for that perfect time. But that perfect time may never come—or it may take a long time. What are you waiting for, really?

Elizabeth Gilbert, in her book *Big Magic*, says that perfectionism is an incarnation of fear, basically another form of fear, dressed up in high heels and makeup. It may look rational on the outside, but underneath there is another fear of not being accepted by others or oneself. I can't disagree with the basics of this notion. We often don't share what we do because we've already decided in our own minds that our work is not perfect yet, and therefore not worthy.

There is a best time to share your work. The author of *Daring Greatly*, Brené Brown, advises sharing your work only after you go through it and feel you're on good terms with it. Having a perfectionist mindset is one thing, but sharing your work without allowing yourself an initial screening is not necessarily healthy either. I found that it wasn't helpful to have a student perform in a recital if they were not prepared and they knew they hadn't practiced sufficiently. They were simply not ready to share as they, as Brené Brown notes, hadn't come to terms with it on their own yet. It doesn't have to be perfectly polished yet, but at the outset, students need to understand and have a conscious awareness about which stages of work they are sharing and what feels like a comfortable environment for sharing their work. Finding that balance between sharing with others to deepen a relationship with what you do and just waiting for the perfect time to come along is not an easy process, yet I promise that it gets better with practice.

I believe that sharing with the world is as important as making your work in the first place. As you are unique to this world, what you create is also unique. Yes, there are many other people who might be doing similar work to yours. But no one else will create in exactly the same way as you do.

Do you know how many millions of classical pianists are out there in this world? Yet, if I went down this rabbit hole of thinking, I wouldn't play piano at all. Why bother playing a piece of music that is three hundred years old and that a million other pianists have already performed? However, no one else would feel or express the music the way I do, as there is only one Jeeyoon. You have to trust and believe that what you express as who you are is another gift to the world, and no one has ever heard or seen what you have to offer. So please come out of your shell and let the world receive it. Do it over and over again. Please don't think this is mere attention-seeking either. I believe that your relationship with what you do should be healthy enough that you love to do it without needing the world to give you any feedback. However, when you have something beautiful, something that you are passionate about, you have a responsibility to release that work to become its own entity rather than only living within you. You will enter a new stage in your relationship with your creation by sharing with others.

What I have learned by being my own agent for years, is that you really need to understand your strength and be able to articulate and analyze it. That is all you need to share. You don't need to rationalize why you are not the best yet or focus on what you perceive as your weakness. Save that for your own growth, in the privacy of your workroom.

> Understand and know your strength, the thing that makes you the most you, then share the process of your work around that. There is only one you in this world.

Imagine a company like Nike. Do you ever hear them talking about their weaknesses or things they need to improve on? Or do you hear them talking about what they are the best at and what they can offer to the world? It is the same with you. Amplify your strength. Create a brand of your own to present yourself to the world with. Practice articulating that strength in a succinct manner. Show your progress and share your thoughts about what you do. Let people join in your playground, too. This act of sharing turns on our sense of connection with people, and also helps us develop a healthier relationship with ourselves.

Imagine you created a beautiful sandcastle on a beach. It may not be the most gorgeous sandcastle ever made by humankind, but you did it on a beautiful afternoon and you were happy doing it. Let's say you share this work with others by taking a picture or talking about it with friends on the beach. Then imagine you created a sandcastle every weekend for six months and shared it with others. Do you think one day someone might come up to you and ask your advice about sandcastles? Do you think your work might make some people smile when they look at it? Do you think your work could help inspire others to create? Do you think you made someone happy as they walked by that sandcastle on the beach? Would these kinds of connections through sharing make you happy also? Would this give you another layer of fulfillment, to know that you added a drop of beauty to the world?

Let's also consider the situation as if this was a sandcastle on an island where no one lives. Say you created a sandcastle every weekend. No sharing, no one to walk by. You were still happy as you created it, though. How would that make you feel differently, compared to a scenario of sharing?

I hope that you can see how you can add another dimension of beauty to your heart and something valuable to the world by simply sharing what you do.

We would like to be a part of this world of yours. Please share what you have just the way it is and let us enjoy the gift that you are in this world. I guarantee that there will always be someone out there who will appreciate your work. If nothing else, in the process of sharing, you will receive the most by deepening your relationship with what you do.

SOMETHING TO THINK ABOUT
WHENEVER YOU'RE READY:

- Ask yourself, "What would I do if there was no possibility of failure?" Then turn this question into "What is worthy of doing even if I fail?" (The first question addresses a perfectionist mindset; the second is the way I would like you to think.)

- After answering the second question, share that thing of yours with others. Take a picture, write a blog, record it in your journal, post a note on social media, share with your friends and family—document the process. You are impacting the world around you in your own way by doing what you love. Start practicing by sharing small with the positive group of people around you. Notice if an act of sharing enhances your experience of your work. Make a mental note. Do it again.

6

PLAY LIKE THE LITTLE CHILD INSIDE OF YOU

*O*ne of my favorite games when I was young was to pretend to make the fanciest and most interesting meal with things I found outdoors—leaves, wildflowers, stones, and dirt. Pebbles became some kind of imaginary veggies, dirt became spices, and wildflowers made lovely side dishes. I could play that way forever, creating something out of nothing. I also remember that I loved inserting a secret message for my mom with clue after clue, hiding a little note with the next clue location in different places in the house. Then, when she found it, she needed to put the mystery sentence back together with some kind of code I'd created. Perhaps I put forth all that effort to say something like "Let's go swim in the ocean this Sunday." I had so much fun creating those notes with my seven-year-old brain, thinking about where to hide them and how to make them trickier to decode.

We were all creative when we were children. When we become adults, we often lose that carefree ability to play—to make something out of nothing. We often try to fit ourselves into society's customs or guidelines in a rigid, conforming way. What happened to that playful, curious child?

I decided to include a user manual in my albums, somewhat like the instructions you would get with the purchase of an electronic device. In the classical music world, CDs are almost sacred; in those insert notes, you would normally put a serious note about each piece, or a bit of history, or some background information. But I wanted to break that mold and find a way to make classical music albums more engaging. I often thought the barrier keeping people away from classical music was in its delivery, not its contents. The user manual to my album reads "Ideally, even if only once, this is how I hope you will listen to my album, *10 More Minutes*." The instructions that I gave for those CDs were not novel, earthshaking ideas, but simply asked listeners to follow four steps with the help of a descriptive image for each step: 1. find a quiet place and allow one hour to listen, 2. use high-quality, closed-ear headphones (or borrow headphones from a friend), 3. read the program notes for each piece, 4. then close your eyes and enjoy. Many people found this approach to a classical album rather refreshing and fun. Often some mentioned to me that they'd never been instructed to listen to an album in any way, saying that it was their first time to listen to music in a focused manner, and not as mere background noise for casual listening.

> We all have a treasure hidden within us. It's called creativity.

It all started because I was curious. Could I connect better with listeners by inviting them into my playground of music with that curiosity in mind? What I learned is something that is actually one of the great magic formulas for life in general, as far as my opinion is concerned: make tasks into a fun game and add a dash of meaning.

I always found radio intriguing when I was growing up, listening to it every night before bed. The intimate relationship the listener builds with the host was quite enchanting to me. One day, after finishing an interview about my recent album, *Over. Above. Beyond.*, as part of the publicity process with *Classical Podcasts* with Lew Smoley, a small, random idea just came into my mind: What if I created my own podcast? Of course, I had no idea how to create a podcast, what equipment I would need, or if I could even

> A great formula for
> life = Fun + Meaning

do it. Without giving the idea deep consideration, I moved on to the next thing on my agenda.

Then something interesting happened. When I had extra time, I slowly started to find myself researching about starting a podcast. I read about it, listened to other people's stories, thought about what content I would like to create if I had one, which microphone to buy, what sort of podcast title I would choose . . . It was like I was stepping onto a huge playground and I was just barely starting to learn how to play with each new toy. Once I decided to give more action to the idea of starting a podcast, the very first thing I did was choose a title. I named it *Journey Through Classical Piano*. I approved it with a smile. "That sounds good," I thought. Then I created a competition for the cover art design with a company called 99designs. There I could have many wonderful graphic designers enter to win "Jeeyoon's best podcast artwork competition" with my own description and criteria. Oh, you don't even know how much fun I had with this!

As of now, fast-forwarding about a year since that initial thought, I have a solid fanbase of about three thousand listeners from all over the world. I always start each podcast saying, "I believe classical music is for everyone, so let's start listening together!" *That* was my reason for launching this fun activity: I wanted to create a bridge between classical music and people from all walks of life. I wanted to make it more approachable and friendly—and to do so by making it fun and giving it meaning.

While those two things, fun and meaning, are equally important in this formula, fun is rooted in our creative souls, that inner child that we all have. Often, we cover it up with the seriousness of adulting and all of its associated responsibilities and attitudes, and we end up neglecting that inner child's needs. I believe that we all can cultivate this part of ourselves, our nature of needing to create just a little more each day. I once watched an interview of Potato Jet, a popular YouTuber who had gotten big for reviewing tech gear. In Potato Jet's interview, he said he started to create his channel as he found himself watching lots of YouTube videos all day long, finally telling himself that if he was going to spend that much time on it, why not create his own rather than simply consuming other people's works? I thought that was an interesting perspective. If you could keep a ratio of doing versus passively receiving at about 7:3 or 8:2, it would be a great step into being more creative. Think about your life right now. What is your ratio of doing versus passive consuming?

You might have to train yourself to be able to listen to your inner child. It is there, in each of us, waiting for us to invite them to play.

I find that being creative may not necessarily relate to your day job. The important thing is to listen to your inner child with a sense of curiosity. That inner child's voice is often so hidden, you may have to put a huge amplifier next to it to be able to hear it. But it's there. We all have it. When I first came up with the idea for that podcast, it all started with just a random thought that popped up out of nowhere, saying, "What if I create my own podcast?" almost sounding crazy at the time. But eventually I paid attention to that voice, as I found myself thinking about it over and over again. I found myself doing research. It was almost like that voice was chasing me so I would notice it and pay more attention. I often woke up in the middle of the night, and that idea was still there. I finally gave in and did something about it. Curiosity led me from one thing to another, then another, then another. I had a good amount of time following up on this curiosity, and I channeled it into playful fun. As Daniel H. Pink says in his book *Drive*, "Make a work into a play, a play into a work." That is a great place to be, right?

The secret?

It always has to start from your own small voice, and no one else's.

Pay attention to yourself carefully. Is there anything, *anything* that you are simply curious about? Even if it sounds silly or small, listen to it and go there. Let your inner child lead you. What other things would you like to try or learn about next? Then go there. Spend some time with it. Have a date with yourself.

Even with basic or mundane tasks, you can add more fun and creativity into the mix. When you go to a grocery store, simply ask yourself, "What if I took a different route today?" and enjoy the difference. Don't get hung up on negatives— for example, even if that route is not the most efficient

> Have fun. Laugh. Don't take it too seriously. Make mistakes. Play wildly in life's playground. Be open. Be curious.

way. The key is that you are throwing yourself into a new experience and enjoying the process. This is a little exercise that we do to keep our inner child speaking up more loudly every day. What if you change one ingredient of your cooking today, and see how the meal comes out differently? Laugh if something doesn't turn out as you wished. Don't take it too seriously. Remember, it is a game of life that you are playing, and curiosity doesn't tag along with judgment. Be open. Have fun.

I read an article somewhere that being stuck in an airport due to a flight delay is actually beneficial to our brain, as we don't do enough daydreaming. When there is no internet access, no meeting to attend, no phone call to make, being stuck in a place like an airport can get us to do the very thing that we all need to do more of: simply do nothing but daydream. Watch the clouds come and go, watch people walk by, just be there, still and calm and present. Then, you just might be able to hear your inner child. That child might be saying, "I would like to do . . ." or "I am curious about . . ."

Give yourself permission to do nothing sometimes, then also permission to be curious, to be loose, to make mistakes, to laugh, and to have fun. Follow and listen to that voice. Every day, that inner child is there, waiting to play with you, if you allow yourself to listen.

Let's play.

You have to allow your inner voice to talk.
If you are busy talking or doing, there is
no chance for it to talk to you.

SOMETHING TO TRY WHENEVER YOU'RE READY:

- Is there anything you are interested in now? Anything? Spend time learning more about that or have fun doing it.

- Go to a park and sit on a bench one day. Just enjoy watching people or nature, or do nothing. Daydream.

- Change up a routine on purpose. Change the way you cook a certain meal. Experiment with a new walking path. Observe the new scenery with a sense of curiosity.

- *Do* things. Don't be just a passive receiver. Walk, read, talk, teach, explain, plant, write, organize, create, play, exercise, draw, record, meet, and build! Your inner child will be happy that you finally took some time to play.

PAGODAS BY CLAUDE DEBUSSY

Whenever I go to New York City, I love to visit the Museum of Modern Art, even when I have just thirty minutes. One of my favorite paintings to stand in front of is *Water Lilies* by Claude Monet. The painting depicts the flower garden at his home, and this was the main focus of his work in the last thirty years of his life. This amazing artwork always makes me feel humble in relation to my own artistic endeavors, knowing he spent decades on this art, and it gives me a positive and peaceful energy. Even though I was never a great painter, every time I play something by the French composer Claude Debussy, I feel like I become a great painter with notes. I color snowy steps with a certain group of notes, then I create the sound of rain and a rainbow with another set of colors. One individual stroke of the brush by an Impressionist painter like Monet may not indicate anything independently, but it becomes a part of the greater whole. For me, Debussy's music is always a fun bit of play on my piano playground.

The first movement from his *Estampes* (which means *prints* in French) is called "Pagodas." A pagoda is a Buddhist or Hindu temple with multitiered layers, often found in East Asia. Debussy was surprised to hear the sounds of East Asia for the first time when he attended a World's Fair called the 1900 Paris Exposition, and he composed many pieces depicting East Asia.[6] I can vividly remember seeing those pagoda-style Buddhist temples on a nearby mountain where I grew up in South Korea. In my memory, it was often covered in a misty morning fog and the smell of pine trees, and I heard a faint gong sound every hour, indicating the time of day.

I am surprised when I play this piece and feel how vividly Debussy could describe my memory of Korea without him ever visiting there. When I play his "Pagodas," I am able to travel back to my youth, to those mountains in that magical time in Korea.

Have you ever been to Asia? Have you ever seen those pagodas in those Buddhist temples? Have you ever hiked in Asia? Do you know the smell of pine trees? Have you ever heard the sound of the gong from those temples?

What I absolutely adore about this movement is the fact that I can take you to somewhere in Asia immediately. The opening chords are like a misty morning, then you walk through a path on the mountain, hearing a gong from far away and then quietly viewing the structure of the temple—the pagoda—from afar. Everything about this moment is peaceful and ethereal. Let me take you on a journey to South Korea with "Pagodas." You don't need a passport for this trip; simply join in with me.

Please go to my podcast, *Journey Through Classical Piano*, Season 1, Episode 11, to listen to it.

---

6   I like this biography of Claude Debussy: *Debussy: A Painter in Sound* by Stephen Walsh.

To listen to the piece and learn more about it, scan here ▶

MOVEMENT #4

Connect with Yourself, Others, and the Universe

1

MEET YOURSELF FIRST

At a difficult period in my life, I had the privilege to meet a great therapist, Dr. Bill. We met every week for more than two years, and he helped me get through those dark times, regain some strength, and ease back into normalcy. I often wished that I had a manual to follow or some magic key that worked every time I came up against obstacles in my life. Instead, I felt quite alone, adrift without answers. These dark moments had nothing to do with music or piano, but came about from broken relationships with myself or others. The source of my pain came from the heartbreak of losing someone, grief, or wounds from the cruelty of another human.

I used to think therapists helped individuals who were suffering with serious mental problems. Then there I was, in that period of my life when I couldn't get by without a weekly dose of talking with Dr. Bill. Some weeks, I counted the hours until I could see him. I may have looked healthy to the world, but inside I was severely wounded and directionless. I now value how a great therapist can help one see oneself more objectively and make changes within. Dr. Bill had a Jedi master look about him and listened to me carefully, always giving me some-thing to think about regarding my thought process. His cat often sat next to me during our conversation and demanded some attention, which always made me smile.

> I find meeting with a great therapist helps one positively. They help you see some parts of yourself more objectively, and this helps you figure out a new direction.

Dr. Bill told me once in a gentle voice, and rather slowly, "Jeeyoon, take up your space in the world. You deserve a space as much as oth-ers." I often asked him, "What do you mean?"—asking question after question. Even after more than two years of conversations, I felt I was still somewhat in a gray area, and there was something I still needed to figure out. I think in many ways, I wanted answers to be black and white, clearly yes or no, or this or that. Instead, life has always been lived on a wide spectrum between yes and no. It may be fifty-five percent yes, but then there are other things to consider—much more complicated and difficult than I imagined. The hardest thing was to break my own patterns and start something new completely. I often asked him, "Please just tell me what to do." But he would smile back at me and tell me, "You already know what to do. Just do that."

I complained inside that he wouldn't simply tell me what to do. But now I know why: He knew I needed to gain strength on my own and learn how to listen to that small voice inside me, developing my own compass within. He couldn't have told me what to do even if he had wanted to—it was something I had to do on my own. He chal-lenged my way of thinking and the way I viewed past events, and after a while I could finally see or understand those events through a different lens. I needed to take the time to make this shift.

It is a relief to know that I've learned from those lessons and that I don't have to go through the same lessons again. As long as I learn what these lessons have to teach, I've found that life doesn't seem to throw the same challenges at me, over and over again. Though I must say, the next challenge that comes my way always seems to be something new that I didn't expect. A big sigh moment indeed! I hope that eventually, at some point in my life, I will run out of lessons to be learned.

I believe we don't fully understand ourselves because we are always changing and evolving. Once, someone asked me if I could go back to my teenage years or my early twenties, would I go there or not. I answered in a heartbeat. "NO WAY!" That would mean I would have to go back to a time when I had less understanding of who I am and how I am. Those difficult life lessons that I finally learned would need to be repeated. That sounds rather scary. During the forty years I have spent on this planet, my life has rewarded me with that much deeper understanding of my soul within me. I have become stronger and have collected tools that will help me know what to do in case of an emergency in life. In those crisis moments, I go through my personal toolbox in the hope that something might work. And more often than not, something does help, as over the years those tools have been discovered and proven to work only for me.

> The hardest part in life is to be able to see the big picture. Unless you change something about it now, it won't be different 10 years from now.

When nothing works, though, I know it is time for another lesson, as I have something I need to learn—I just have to figure out what that is sooner rather than later. I've learned that unless I change myself, the root of a certain issue never just goes away magically. Simply avoiding it would cause another painful life lesson at some point or an unexpected side effect. It's worth the price to face the problem head-on and when it arises, rather than avoiding it and hoping it will go away.

Neil Pasricha, in his book, *The Happiness Equation*, says that

"Happiness is when what you think, what you say, and what you do are in harmony." I find that this is very true in my life. Once I decided on my principles, I make sure to adhere to them even when no one is watching me, or when those principles are challenged. Abiding by my principles means I'm being honest and transparent with myself. I never have to hide my true self or wear a mask in front of anyone. I can just be me, always, regardless of what I do, who I meet, or what situation I find myself in. This approach has helped me live a happy and liberating life.

Have your own principles and make a decision to abide by them regardless of how difficult that is. Just be you, keeping healthy boundaries for yourself and the world.

The tricky part has been to determine what precisely those principles are for *me*. What are some of my rules that I would not allow myself or anyone to break? To answer this, I went through a lot of soul searching, failures, long conversations, therapy sessions, and challenges, all which helped me shape those healthy boundaries or principles. These rules are so personal, and I don't believe I've ever shared them with even my closest friends, but I know what they are deep down. When these rules are challenged—which happens often—I am able to tell myself calmly what to do and direct myself to a place of peace, with a reminder of what I believe in. I don't need to rely on what others believe is the right way to live, or what principles to follow. This is up to me. (I think I finally found how to take up my own deserved space in the world, Dr. Bill.)

What I think, what I say, and what I do all line up. That is the only way I would like to strive to live in my life.

The journey of understanding my soul has been not easy, and I know there is much more to discover and learn. But one thing has become clear: I will not do anything to mess up my principles. If there is a conflict within me on a decision or something I am about to do, I may sense that I am stepping into territory that I know I should not cross into. I may hear a small voice within me, or get an uncomfortable feeling. More and more, I am becoming in tune with myself when I am about to violate my own rules, and I'm able to stop myself before going astray. That tool alone probably has saved me from many dramas in my life.

I find that not only understanding my own soul, but also understanding my weaknesses and strengths is critical. What are the areas that I can improve in, and what are the areas I am good at? While I encourage myself to shine with my strengths, I need to keep working on my weaknesses. In order to grow and progress, I've found it's important to hone the ability to give myself feedback—as a type

---

Some challenges in life ask us to cross the line of being you. Don't do that. Regardless of how great it sounds at this moment, you will eventually have to pay the price of being untrue to who you are.

---

of metacognition—so I can become a better version of myself. I need to encourage myself to push the limitless possibilities within me, yet remain clear enough to recognize and work on any weakness holding me back from doing just that.

Whether you like it or not, you are on your own in your unique journey—just you and your soul within you. How much do you know about this person? What do they like? What do they tend to do? What makes them happy? What is one thing they believe, even if it is challenged? What is the best part of this person? What could improve?

What are the things that would coax them out of bed when they're feeling down? What sort of things help when they're discouraged?

> Try to get to know yourself better, in every direction. Then keep working on yourself to be better. You are the only one who can do that.

Make a mental list of all of these things as you move forward in your life. Every time you discover more about yourself or learn a great life lesson, you are just unlocking the next level of this game called life, and you're *a step closer to becoming a better you.*

You and you. That is it.

Just like putting an oxygen mask on yourself first before helping others in case of an airline emergency, you need to establish a good relationship with yourself first before helping others. Use a therapist or mentor when needed, but remember, *you* need to make that first step toward a better you, and it is your responsibility to craft your own tools that you can call on in case of a life emergency. If you seem to repeat negative patterns in your life, chances are you're either not aware of what needs fixing, or you're simply avoiding the problem.

Unfortunately, some issues will always be there unless you do something about them. Choose to meet yourself first and take that step into a better you. It is easier than you might think. You are the only one who can do it.

SOMETHING TO THINK ABOUT
WHENEVER YOU'RE READY:

- Is there anything you want to improve about yourself? What have you done about it? Have you considered talking to a therapist or a mentor? You can always do *something* about it, even if it is small. Also, reading is one of the best ways to keep improving yourself. Try it.

- What are the top 3 things that you know work positively for you when you feel down?

    1. _____

    2. _____

    3. _____

- What are the top 3 principles in your life?

    1. _____

    2. _____

    3. _____

- What makes you laugh?

- What are your tendencies in a relationship with others that you would like to improve?

- What is your best personality trait?

- What are you good at?

- What helps you calm down when you feel angry or frustrated?

- What makes you happy?

2

CHOOSE TO FEEL AND CONNECT WITH OTHERS

"I am swimming in a pond alone in the early evening one summer. A shining reflection of the moon is on the surface of the calm water. There is a sound of crickets and frogs. I hear the peaceful sound of water as I slowly swim, feeling the water caressing me. Everything about this moment is peaceful and magical. That is what I imagine while I play this movement of Schumann, 'In the Evening,' from *Fantasiestücke*, Op. 12. I hope you enjoy it."

A microphone onstage has become the trademark of my concerts. I always share a personal note about each piece before a performance, except at the end of the concert before encores, and I don't walk off stage after each piece, which seems to be standard procedure for classical concerts. These little gestures might be nothing unusual in the theater or at a pop music concert, but this is a bit unorthodox when it comes to the classical piano concert scene. In fact, some concert presenters have asked me if this talking part of my concert was necessary, and I always insisted that it was, saying, "I know music speaks for itself, but this is important to me. I would like to create a better bridge between me and my audience, if at all possible."

Being open to receiving what the music offers is like being an empty vessel waiting to be filled in the best way—and this is the job of an artist. When I play, I am like a cup for the music. People cannot drink the water of a composer unless I hold it intact with my own glass cup. The cup does not have my own signature and does not come in my favorite colors, but rather it is a transparent cup in my own unique shape. My goal is always to express the composer's intention first, and I do that through the unique shape of my glass cup. At the very moment of playing that piece, I am at one with the composer's, my own, and the listeners' souls, and the present time and place melts away.

An audience member came to me one evening after a concert and gave me a handwritten letter. She said it was a love letter to me as she handed it over secretly, asking me to read it later. In my hotel room, I opened it and read: "Dear Jeeyoon, I am not sure how in the world you could do this. But today, your music brought me to my child-hood, where I could touch my mom one more time. I talked with her and touched her. I was having a hard time letting go after my mom's passing three years ago. Today, I could finally let her go during your concert and I am ready to start a new day tomorrow. I can never thank you enough."

Musicians time-travel with music. When I sit down and play piano, I am able to meet a composer who lived 250 years ago, then I relive my youth, then the listeners' past and their future—all through music. This is an absolutely beautiful and fascinating aspect of being a classical pianist. I never experience the same exact thought or image or feelings, even when I play the same pieces. Where I might travel while I per-form a piece of music is something I always look forward to—because it's unknown, a mystery to me, I am excited to reach it. Even though I am the one who performs a piece, the aspect of time travel is a unique journey of its own, each time I perform. The more I allow myself to be vulnerable, the more meaningful journeys I can take.

During piano lessons, what I end up spending the most time on with my students are discussions about how to feel empathy during a certain passage. "What do you feel here? What do you think the composer must have felt? Can you relate to a joyful or sad moment in your life? What kind of story does it make you think of, whether it be your own or someone else's?" I find that playing classical music is all about expressing this ever-searching discovery of raw human emotions. Love, anger, frustration, hope, joy, and sadness all existed three hundred years ago, just as they do now. It is magical to feel connected to another human from three hundred years ago, in a similar way that we would feel now. In music, we feel a composer, we feel a performer, we feel ourselves, we feel our past, we feel other people in our past or present. A story of your past may come into and out of your head, or a new feeling might be transferred through a performance. That is a thrilling aspect of art. I often tell my audience, just before I perform a piece, that we will meet in another dimension, one where space and time don't exist. I literally feel that I meet each one of them, and it happens in such a special way that I cannot begin to describe this experience in words.

> The connection we feel through music is truly magical. It strengthens our inner desire for connections with others.

Often when we are in deep despair over the loss of someone or find ourselves in difficult times, what we want is for others not to say anything or act in a certain way, but to simply feel it together, to exist together in the space of pain.

> We are here to feel connected, to love, to support each other. That is our nature.

This is empathy—feeling what others feel. That's what we long for. Just feeling that someone else can share our pain is often the best way to find solace.

There are two kinds of live performances: one is to present and the other is to connect. In the first model, you get ready for a concert and simply perform or present. It is basically a one-way channel, which is easier in many ways, as there are fewer variables to worry about. The energy is given out by the performer, and the audience simply receives. This type of presentation is a great way to grab the audience's attention—for example, if you need to tell them there's a fire in the building. The crowd doesn't need energy, they just need you to call out. Often my students think that a live performance needs to be done this way. You practice, then go and give a performance.

In reality, I believe that live performances are meant to go deeper by creating connections. The performer and the audience are there to connect, and they're willing to receive, willing to listen, willing to take a risk, and willing to engage with everything about that moment. When I walk on the stage, I am there to talk about music, talk to people, express the music, then receive from the moment both music and people. It is a two-way channel. I believe that is the beauty of a live performance. No matter how many times I perform a particular piece of music, it is played for the first time with each new audience I come before, even if some of the audience members have heard me play it before. You are also in the middle of a live performance—a performance called *life*. Every time you go onto the stage of life, I hope you make an effort to connect, receive, take a risk, and engage in that very moment.

You can always go inside your own cave to regenerate yourself at times when you need to, but make a conscious effort to connect with others when you come out.

I find that this notion of connection and empathy is a tool that we all strive for in life. When I listen to a friend, I watch her eyes and receive her feelings. When I talk to her, I give my thoughts and my emotions. I react to her and she responds. Just like a live performance, we can *choose* this communication to be one-way. Two-way channel interaction is optional, not a default. We can always choose to pretend to listen, not to be engaged, and say only what we want to say, without really allowing the other person to communicate with us.

Are you willing to be connected? Are you listening? Are you really listening?

You may never fully understand someone, but we can always try to feel what they feel, to listen to their story, to share their pain, their joy, and their heartbreak.

Why?

Because we are meant to love one another, to be connected to one another, to support each other, to lift each other up, to listen to each other. Otherwise, life would lose its meaning. I believe that when we are doing what we are meant to do, we finally become who we are meant to become. Fish need water to swim, and we need other humans to live fully. Choose to be connected, choose to have two-way channels with each other, and choose to listen, receive, and give. *I feel you.* Though this may not be easy at times, I think we can always try to be better.

SOMETHING TO THINK ABOUT
WHENEVER YOU'RE READY:

- When you watch a movie or attend a play or read a book, try to feel what it would be like to be one of those characters. Go there deeply, as if you have become that person.

- Think about the hardest day in your life, the most heartbreaking and painful day you went through. Try to remember that feeling. When you know that someone is going through a difficult time, simply imagine they are going through their hardest day too. Feel the pain with them.

- When you have a conversation with anyone, consciously try to hold a two-way channel as much as possible. Listen, react, receive, then give, feel, and connect.

- When you go to a classical concert, try to feel what the composer was feeling when they created that music. Think about what they might have been going through on the day they composed it. Try to feel what the performer feels. Imagine yourself becoming the performer. Let the music take you to a place of raw emotion. If that brings you to a memory of your past, go there and feel it.

3

USE THE POWER OF
POSITIVE WORDS

Mary used to be a student who was reluctant to play piano in front of others, no matter what the circumstances. She would be hard on herself any time she made a mistake, saying, "That was horrible," "I should stop playing piano," "Of course, I will never play like Rubinstein." Interestingly, she was generous toward other people by giving lots of compliments. She always encouraged other students, telling them how much they were improving; she just didn't say the same to herself. She was an A+ student in her school years, and an accomplished woman in her career. Despite her fine ability on piano, she did not even allow herself to practice when her husband was in the house, but only when he was at work. She kept her passion for piano to herself. When fellow piano students complimented her playing, she replied that they were just being nice. On top of that, she would add something like "Oh, you probably didn't catch my huge mistake in the middle part of that Chopin nocturne. That was pretty bad." It was also difficult for her to accept compliments regarding piano. I could envision her blossoming into a beautiful pianist, but she couldn't see herself in that way at all.

One day, during our lessons, I suggested something for her to try. The idea was that if she thought anything negative about herself, she simply could not say it out loud. We may not be able to control what kind of thoughts arise in our heads, but we certainly can choose how we give them power. We have the power to control the words we use.

> Words are powerful. You need to choose how to use this tool for you or against you.

It was difficult for her at first. Automatically, she would have a negative reaction out loud during a lesson or even after a public performance. But I redirected her immediately, reminding her that those words were not something we would like to hear. Since she was genuinely curious and also wanted to progress, the no-negative-words game became our new norm after a while.

Once that became our system, I also encouraged her to say and share out loud any positive thing about her playing. Another rule was that if others complimented her, she needed to accept it fully, without defending or diminishing it. She was to simply accept praise with a simple "thank you" and enjoy the positive emotion that might arise from those words.

> Simply not saying the negative words out loud is the first and one of the most important steps.

It probably took a solid three years until I finally saw a noticeable change in her notion of herself as a pianist. She eventually became a much kinder person to herself. After her first solo piano recital in her late fifties, she said to me, "I am so proud of myself for being able to give a solo recital like that. I enjoyed sharing music with friends and family, and you know what? I did a fantastic job!" To hear these positive words from someone like Mary was indeed a profound moment that I will always remember. We employed many other techniques to get to this point during our study, but I am certain that positive words had a lot to do with this change.

Words have the power to direct our thoughts, emotions, and behaviors. I believe that Mary's growth in her life started when she stopped saying negative words out loud. How many times do we say those negative words to ourselves and to others every day? Do you know? Have you ever listened and counted them? Often, we don't even realize when we say those words. We unconsciously allow those toxic words to give power over our minds. Saying negative things out loud gives power to that negativity. On the other hand, when you don't say the negatives out loud, that means you are simply acknowledging them within your mind, but not letting them grow. That is the first step and one of the most critical steps to a real change.

I have a rule about words that you may have heard a version of but never really paid attention to: When there is nothing good to say, simply don't say anything out loud. If you have something good to say, don't be shy about it. Express it fully. I encourage myself and others whenever possible with positive words. I am extremely

> Splurge with positive words. Express it fully. Don't hold it back.

intolerant with negative words being said out loud, not only to myself or to others, but also hearing them from others. But don't confuse this with constructive and healthy feedback that I give during lessons. That's different, as it's rooted in a positive-growth mindset and comes from a place of love.

I'm talking here about avoiding negative words that don't have any other purpose than expressing ugliness or venting insecurities, urges, and primal angst not channeled out in a healthy way—this includes curses, insults, sarcastic criticism, and of course gossip. I know that I can't control what others do or say, but in my world, I believe that if something would be unkind to say in front of a particular person, it is also not good to say behind that person's back. You might think that it's no big deal to talk about another person lightly when socializing over a cocktail. But I believe strongly that these wasted negative words bring toxic energy back to oneself, damaging the gossiper more than the one gossiped about. Plus, if gossip is the only thing available to you when you're with certain people, I would seriously rethink the fundamental relationships with those people in the first place. Life is too short to be wasted.

My student Tina told me that she was absolutely elated when she got a text message from a fellow piano student during her virtual piano recital on a Zoom call during COVID-19. The text said, "Tina, you are killing it! Wow, way to go!" Apparently, the text came through while Tina was sharing her prerecorded performance of an all-time favorite classical piece, Debussy's "Arabesque." Nearly fifty virtual audience members on Zoom cheered for her afterward. Tina told me she thought about that specific text message thousands of times in her head, and that this gave her a huge dose of encouragement that lasted throughout the following week. She asked, "Isn't that weird that I loved that text so much?"

I can completely relate to Tina, understanding the positive effects of words. At my concerts, I put out a guest book at the entrance of the concert hall, where audience members can leave a message for me after the performance. Mostly, they compose one or two sentences about the concert and their experience. I always want to meet as many audience members as possible in person, but in reality, it is almost impossible to meet all of them in a meaningful way individually after the concert is over. There is only just enough time to shake hands and to exchange a few words. Then, when the crowds disappear and I'm alone in my quiet hotel room, I love reading those comments in that guest book. One by one, I savor each of them, smiling and feeling the same effect that my student, Tina, felt after receiving that text message.

> Words have such power to encourage and lift one's spirits. Use them for yourself and for others.

All of those little notes and kind words from many of my concerts became my energy pack, which I revisit whenever I need a dose of encouragement or I'm feeling down. Isn't that weird? It's just words, right? How is it that such a simple thing like a few words could deliver such invigorating strength and power? This is an incredible tool and also easy for any of us to access. You know what else? It costs nothing— it's absolutely free.

If you want to try to invite that superpower into your life, I have a suggestion. Simply be a person who says positive words—to others, and to yourself. Encourage people. Splurge. Don't be stingy with encouragement. If you want to be encouraged and supported, then hand out your stores of those positive words first. This is all about expressing love, exercising love, and receiving love.

The Bible instructs us to love one another, love your neighbors as much as you love yourself.

Let's talk to ourselves with the same kindness we would show to someone whom we love. Let's be that first person who can shower someone with compliments and encouragement. We all have the power to make this world a better, more positive place.

It starts with what we say in each moment.

It's your choice.

SOMETHING TO TRY
WHENEVER YOU'RE READY:

- Be highly aware of anything you say today. Count how many times you speak negatively toward yourself or to others.

- Try simply not say anything negatively to yourself or to others for the next week or month—or even a year. You might have those words in your head, but just don't say them out loud.

- At every opportunity, say out loud positive and encouraging words to yourself and to others. (Texting is also a form of saying things out loud.) Splurge with it. Of course, don't be artificial, but when you feel any positive feeling toward something, express it fully!

- Write positive and encouraging words to yourself in a diary. Keep practicing until those words become natural to your hand and your ear.

- Make your own energy bomb scrapbook where you can collect nice cards that you received or printed-out emails or texts from the past that you want to reread whenever you feel down or feel negative. (Remember, you always have a chance to be that person who can give that energy bomb to someone else.)

4

DON'T DO IT ALONE

*T*he piano is an instrument that can stand alone in concerts as an independent, solo instrument. Even though a piano can be incorporated alongside other instruments, or as part of an orchestra, no other instrument can function alone so independently and beautifully as well as a piano does. It has the power to imitate a full orchestra but also has the most sensitive and intimate voice quality. It is such a fascinating instrument, with its chameleon-like versatility in various possibilities.

Sometimes people like to generalize about a person's personality based on which instrument they play, such as diva opera singers or laid-back trumpet players, and so on. Solo pianists are often characterized as introverts who can work for countless hours without seeing any other human for days. Although that's a bit of a generalization, it is not surprising to me that quarantining from COVID-19 didn't bother me all that much or affect my workflow or daily practice schedule. After all, I'm used to working, performing, practicing, and traveling alone. The key for me is to be independent and do mostly solo work, but not to be isolated. Luckily, I manage to keep that balance of isolation as a performing artist by being a teacher also, and meeting with my wonderful students on a regular basis.

What I found interesting was that my students, who are also pianists, have a similar independent character. They would have been just fine working with me in a private lesson without meeting other students. That is why I created group classes, in order to go against these isolation tendencies in piano, so they could meet with each other outside of their own private lessons. I find that, in a community, we feel a sense of belonging, gain support from others, and become contributors to the wider community. During group classes, we discuss challenges, talk about books we've read, play for each other, and share music together. We also have regular piano parties three times a year, which are basically piano recitals by my adult students where they share their music with other guests and each other. After the performance portion of the party, we always end with a potluck and then socialize afterward.

> Being independent and being isolated are two different things. Be happily alone, but also find a way to stay connected.

Engaging with fellow learners who have the same interest of piano and a growth mindset creates a positive environment so we can learn from each other by watching others' successes and struggles. The students not only encourage each other's study, but also help create an environment where it's okay to take a risk while learning. They are all alone in their journey of learning piano, but being connected within a community helps them overcome obstacles.

> A positive community that can help you learn from and support each other is very important.

Before each piano party, I often go to the front and tell the audience, "In a marathon, you can't run for the runners, but you can always cheer for them. Being on a stage requires tremendous courage and vulnerability. Your cheers and big applause will help each of the performers tonight gain that extra boost when they begin their journey of performing." Then I practice applauding with the audience, cheering as loudly as possible, full of positive energy. When each student finishes their pieces, everyone cheers, "Way to go! . . . Beautiful! . . . Bravo! . . . Brava!" with huge applause. I can imagine how each of my students might feel at that very moment, in getting that kind of intense feedback and energy from the audience. It really helps.

Life is not easy. There are not only countless failures and trials, but also daily battles in our minds. If you are in an environment where you are surrounded by negative people, your life journey will have unnecessary weight added on top of it, making it harder than it should be. Imagine that you are working on a challenging project that you are excited about. When you share that with a friend of yours, you hear, "That sounds really difficult. That would be almost a miracle if it works. Not many projects like that have succeeded in the past." If you keep hearing that over and over again, I bet that you would probably end up agreeing that this project is indeed impossible. Compare that scenario with another friend of yours who says, "Wow. That sounds fantastic! I can't wait to hear more about it. I bet no one thought of that angle yet! How unique!"

Which one made you feel more energized? Which one gave you the courage to keep pushing forward? Without any external pulling from others, we are already fighting against our own negative voices. Why would we add more obstacles in life when we are continually trying to overcome those already in the way?

Without external negative voices, life is still heavy. Choose an environment that lifts you up in your life's journey. Be around people whom you admire.

Choose a community that has positive energy. Gather people around you who want the best from you and encourage you. Choose to be around people whom you admire and want to be like. Choose to be close with positive people. On the other hand, limit your contact with people who say negative things about the world and the future. Choose not to share your passion with those who are judgmental and jealous. We all have different facets in our lives. You may belong to many different groups associated with various activities, such as tennis, book club, swimming, a religious group, or related to your hobby. Some groups may be seasonal—coming in a certain time of your life and then you move on. You may find a certain group is not a good fit for you after you join them. Don't stay with the group out of a feeling of obligation. You will be a better member of the community when you feel you belong and have your reason for being there. Be intentional about choosing a community that brings out the best in you.

If you can't find the kind of community you want, start a new one on your own. Two or three people is a good start. Why not? Maybe you aren't a people person and are fine with being alone. Trust me. I understand being an introvert. That's actually the best reason to look for or create a community. When I found the right community, my introvert side shined in the group, as I gained a sense of belonging to the world around me and was able to contribute with what I could do. That sense of connection was rewarding and meaningful for me.

When my student Steve was too discouraged to work on a piece of music and missed our piano party, he got emails, cards, and text messages from fellow students, saying he was missed and we looked forward to seeing him soon. A lot of students shared some of their own stories of struggles they faced in their own music journeys. When Molly's husband was in the hospital, fellow students sent flowers and notes, wishing for a quick recovery. It is a community for piano, but it isn't only about piano. It is about a valuable human connection between people who genuinely want to encourage and support each other's journey through life.

When I walked onstage at my concert in San Diego for my CD release, I heard the crowd applauding and cheering more loudly and enthusiastically than usual. I felt as though each of my fifteen piano students had impacted the hundreds of audience members in a very positive way. As I bowed to the audience, I smiled big. Without this community that I have created, my career as a performing artist would have been much harder and quite lonely. Sure, I give concerts in other cities to an enthusiastic group of people in the audience as well. But they may come to a concert once and then leave, often never to be heard from again.

This aspect of being a performer could leave me feeling lonesome, even after the most amazing con-certs in front of thousands of people.

A positive community encourages you to take a risk and go for it.

However, because I have cultivated a group in my community, these people stay with me, willing to go on my life journey with me, just as I'm willing to be a part of their lives. Life as a solo artist can feel isolating, unless artists consciously create a core community around them. It doesn't have to be a large group—two to five people could be a great number.

We are on our own journey through life, but it is much easier and more fun when we are surrounded by other positive forces. Choose or create a positive community that helps you thrive and supports you, so that you feel safe in taking risks that will help you advance with confidence.

With these communities, you will feel that a forward current is being created underneath your boat. All of a sudden, your rowing gets much lighter and easier. When you feel tired, you can just depend on those currents that were created by others, and let yourself flow until you are able to row hard again. They are there for you and you are there for them. Doesn't that sound comforting?

Don't row alone.

SOMETHING TO TRY WHENEVER YOU'RE READY:

- When you talk to a friend or a colleague about their projects, the best help you can give them is to support and encourage their efforts. You can't live their life. But you can cheer them on their journey.

- Take a look at who you meet regularly. Are they positive? Are they a group of people who strive to be better in their lives? Do you have anyone whom you look up to? We can't change who we have as our family members or coworkers, but we do have control over many of the people we choose to share our life with. Choose to meet a group of people who have positive energy and avoid negative people.

- Join a group that has similar interests and good energy. When you don't have any group that you click with, try to create your own. Who would be a great ally to help your amazing group get started?

- Be the person whom you want to be around. Be that friend you want to have as a friend first. When you want to receive something, whether that's positive words, texts, emails, calls, or to spend time together, give that to your friends first.

5

TALKING TO STRANGERS

"*Jeeyoon*, practice exchanging small talk with strangers, like in a gas station." That is what my therapist recommended about eleven years ago. And that was when I finally recognized that I was wounded. If I had been healthy, such a suggestion should not have been difficult for me to follow through on. More to the point, if I had been healthy, a suggestion like this would never have been made. I had pulled myself back from the world and was reluctant to connect with anyone that I didn't know. In those difficult times, I was not being my usual self—the person who likes to connect with others. I was afraid of being hurt and fearful of the unknown.

Talking to a stranger means you are putting yourself out there, showing a willingness to make a connection. When you see them, they also see you. What I've learned about these light interactions is that we are allowing others to experience us, and we're also opening our hearts to receive them. These interactions may include saying hello to a person on the street, or having a little chat in a grocery line. However fleeting or outwardly inconsequential, they open two-way channels that make our souls shine together in those moments. I believe that wishing a stranger well, or holding a good thought for a person you don't know, are opportunities for us to function with goodness, as compassionate human beings. That simple act of making a small connection may make big butterfly ripples in our hearts, reminding us that we belong to this earth and are contributing to the world in a way that we may not be able to see right away but may wish to explore.

"Do you go to this concert series by this organization often?" I asked an elderly lady sitting next to me as we sat in the audience waiting for a chamber music concert to begin. Initially I felt resistant to talking to her, but I introduced myself anyway and made a little small talk. She told me she comes to this concert series whenever she can, and her best friend, who is now in the hospital recovering from a recent hip surgery, first recommended that she come to this concert about two years ago. She also mentioned that she likes any concert that includes the piano. I smiled back at her, saying "Me too." When the concert was over, the lady told me with a big smile that it was lovely to meet me and to share my company during the concert. I was glad that I'd made an effort to talk to her despite my initial resistance.

Just like that, I practiced talking to strangers, little by little. At a concert, grocery store, and café, I talked to strangers without any intention other than simply to connect in a light manner, and it always turned out better than I anticipated and left me with something positive afterward.

Apparently, there was another reason my therapist recommended I try this. Recently, I heard Laurie Santos, an associate professor of psychology at Yale University, on her podcast *The Happiness Lab*, say that talking to strangers helps one feel happier and more positive. Then she added that most people, however, whether they are introverts or extroverts, always anticipate that talking to a stranger might not turn out as well as it does. Introverts, especially, might dread having to talk to a stranger in a situation like on a plane or bus. Yet even those introverts find that most of the time it does make them feel good inside afterward.

I can totally relate to this notion, as I am more of an introvert. I do find that talking to strangers is actually wonderful after all, and it gets a bit easier the more I do it. These days, before I even know it, it feels like I am reaching out my hand to them and asking them how they are doing, or saying "Hello" in a meaningful way.

I always love going to a farmers' market, probably because I grew up with that kind of culture in Korea, where I used to buy fresh vegetables and fruits from street vendors that sell directly from their own farms. They always knew which fruits or vegetables were good that week and recommended accordingly. I remember one of the strangest things in grocery stores in the United States when I first arrived was to see grapes all year round, and not only during specific months. When I used to go to a fruit store near my grandmother's house, which was about fifteen minutes away from my home in Korea, in order to get some fruit for her before my visit, the store guy recognized me, and said, "Granny got good pears earlier this week, why don't you get some mountain berries today? She loves those and this only lasts for this week." It was like an extended family; that little connection we had back then felt like genuine care and love.

> Apparently, talking to a stranger makes one happier. Isn't that interesting? It is a nice byproduct.

Today when I go to farmers' markets, I talk to farmers, asking questions about their produce and their farms. Obviously, these are not life discussions, but just simple moments for chatting. I find myself worrying about their farms when I see there are big storms coming into town, and I wish them well. They may think of me when I don't show up all of a sudden for months after going there every week. They have no idea about what I do or even what my name is. Do we need to know what we do or where we are from in order to connect, though? I sometimes wonder if anything would change between us if they recognized me as a pianist when they happened to see me in concert. I somehow think that it would not make a bit of difference to them— or to me. What I do is not who I am. But still I, my soul, feels truly connected with them, in those brief moments when we talk.

> What I do is not who I am.

Connecting in this way has been difficult with COVID-19. On the street, we don't exchange handshakes. We limit eye contact. We keep that six feet of social distance. The very thing we long for—connection as human beings—was the very cause of the vicious virus. We push, then we pull. We want to push people away to protect ourselves, then we long to pull them back to feel connected.

Yet it's interesting to me that I've made so many conscious efforts during this pandemic to be connected with others, as my need to connect has been stronger than ever. I made an effort to talk to a friend whom I hadn't talked with for a while and did it through Zoom and over coffee. I wrote a long email to a teacher in Japan from my university years that I meant to reconnect with. I made phone calls to my mom in Korea more often than usual. I started a bi-weekly newsletter, and I started live streaming on my YouTube channel to talk

> Making an effort to be connected with others is a choice. I hope you choose that.

with people I don't know. What I found interesting was that as soon as I replied back to those comments from my videos with a real intention of connecting with the person behind the computer, most of the time those people became very real, excitedly wishing to connect back with me. All of these efforts could have seemed like more of a hassle to me, or felt more task-like, in other circumstances, but this pandemic, just like talking to a farmer or a lady sitting next to me at a concert, has taught me that these efforts for connections with people make me feel more alive, and I have received so much from feeling these connections. Connecting with strangers has stayed in my heart for a long time, like a beautiful little shooting star.

How about you? How are you? How are you really doing today? I hope you are having a good day. I put you in the palm of my hand now and wish you well at this very moment. I wish for you an inner peace and joy.

It may feel unnecessary to talk to strangers most of the time, especially if you are an introvert. But I urge you to try it as an experiment. It could be a simple hello, or a smile, or random silly things that don't matter at all. Make a mental note for that afterward. Was it horrible indeed? Was it nice after all? How did it make you feel? Imagine that the small gesture creates a spark of electric light that shines every time you talk to a stranger. You are letting the world know that you see them, they see you, you wish them well, and they wish you well.

That is a connection that may not matter much in that moment, but in the big picture, the earth would look like a beautiful shining Milky Way with those lights that we create if we all chose to enter these little shining moments more often.

SOMETHING TO TRY
WHENEVER YOU'RE READY:

- When you are in a line, try to talk to the person behind you or to the cashier. Asking a quick light question is a great way to start. Or look at them, smile, and say "Hi!" Complimenting others is also a great way to break the ice.

- Every time you pass someone when you take a walk, make sure to say hi with a smile. Take the time to say hello to their pets when appropriate.

- Taking it to the next level . . . When you are in a plane or taxi or Uber or bus, or perhaps just in a waiting room, start a conversation with someone. That person might respond coldly, or this might be the best conversation you ever have. You simply don't know. Experiment for yourself.

- Always make a mental note if conversations with strangers light you up afterward. Think about how much better your contact with them was than you initially assumed or expected it would be. Make sure to do it again, allowing this to become part of your lifestyle.

- Visualize that every time you connect with anyone, it electrifies you positively. Remember the image of the sparkling Milky Way.

6

EXPRESS YOURSELF
THROUGH WHAT YOU DO

*E*very time I give a concert or play the piano, I am using one of those five love languages, the one referred to as "acts of service," according to Gary Chapman in his book *The Five Love Languages*. I am expressing my love of music to myself and to others by using music as a tool to connect and lift one's spirits. I find that everything we do has the ability to express our inner intention without words. Cooking for your family is to show your love for them, calling my mom is to show her that I am thinking of her, holding a door open for the person behind is to show that you care for them, and using less plastic is to show the earth that you care for the environment. Each action we take reflects who we are and what we believe. It can be direct or indirect—such as how you spend your money, which reveals your intentions and shows that you're being generous to others.

My grandfather used to tell me that if you want to know someone, just take a look at where and how they spend their money. I never quite understood what he meant. I have to admit that I didn't like the fact that it made me feel a bit guilty, thinking I could always do better. When I did my initial crowdfunding campaign for my first album, *10 More Minutes*, I was surprised to learn how difficult it is to ask for money. As much as I was excited about the project, it felt like I was asking too much for people to participate by donating money. I had to practice in my closet hundreds of times before I was able to ask—out loud—for a donation in person. I asked everyone I knew to be a part of the journey of my album, telling them I could not do this alone. It was such a humbling experience. To my surprise and thankfulness, the project was successfully funded in the end.

What I loved most was that each donation had a letter attached to it, with a sentiment like "This sounds great. I love your music. I can't wait to have your vision of this project realized, and I am behind you to support your music." It was such a valuable learning moment for me to see how money had the ability to express love and support, as I experienced when I received it.

You see, for a long time, I was not in a position where I could help anyone with money, as I struggled to cover my bare minimum as a poor international student. When things improved and I became able to help others, I found that it was such a privilege to be able to do that. It is as powerful to be a giver as a receiver. Helping someone else feels like I am helping a past version of myself—the younger Jeeyoon. I find that being generous with money has

> Being able to help is a privilege. It is such a powerful way to live life.

a strong message, if one can afford doing it. If someone is starving, that person needs food more than anything else. Simply hearing condolences such as "I am sorry that you are hungry. That must be difficult" would be nice, but not very helpful.

Empathy requires us to feel what others feel, but compassion requires taking action with regard to that feeling of empathy. Oftentimes, skipping the kind words in this case, and simply giving the person in need food or money, is what is truly needed. I have never experienced being homeless, nor have I suffered from starvation or some other disaster, but I can only imagine how I might feel if I were desperately in need, and someone finally came along and helped me. That would feel like a gift from heaven.

Now I have a little better sense of what my grandfather was saying. It does tell you a great deal about someone if you see their bank account statement. If they spend money on concert tickets, they must like live performances and support the arts. If they spend money on garden tools, they must be into gardening. If they spend money for a personal trainer, they must think exercise is important. If they support the Humane Society, they must have a soft feeling toward animals. Spending money is another action that we do based on what we believe and who we are.

If you spend time with your art or craft project, you are expressing your interest by doing it. If you spend time watching environmental documentaries, that means you are curious and support preserving the natural environment. What does your action say about you? Does it say what you'd like it to say? The cumulative picture of your actions reflects who you are and who you want to become. An action speaks louder than words sometimes. Try to be aware of what you do on a daily basis and remember that what you do reflects what you believe.

> Your actions say who you are. Make sure they are in line with what you believe.

Just like exercising, being generous requires some training. I am in the process of that training also. Some of you might be a beginner, or some of you might already be pros at giving. When you complete an act of giving and being generous, you open your palm. That open hand now can be filled with other valuable things that come back to you. In order to receive, you need to open up. Closed fists aren't capable of receiving. I found that one doesn't automatically become a giver simply because they have money. It requires a conscious thought or decision about who you want to become or how you want to live your life. That decision leads to action.

I suggest that you start with something small like donating ten dollars to an organization whose cause you support. If and when you can't afford to, think about some ways to help others by doing. It doesn't have to be anyone far away either, and it can be a family member or friend that you see needs assistance. Let your actions speak from your heart. Decide who you want to become, then make sure that your words and actions say the same thing.

> Remember that by giving, you receive. The closed fist can't receive anything.

I send a wishful message to people through my music. Hopefully, because of the magical power in music, someone in an audience might feel lighter and stronger after a concert. They may feel renewed and healed. I do what I can do with the piano to express love and care to others, because I want to be a compassionate person.

Do you know the secret though? By giving whatever that would be, music or money or something else, I always feel that I receive more than I give. I feel connected when I've contributed and helped others with my intention, which gives me a great sense of satisfaction.

Try it. It's a gift you can give to the whole world, and also to yourself.

SOMETHING TO TRY
WHENEVER YOU'RE READY:

What do you support? Animal rights? Justice against race discrimination? Green environment? Performing arts?

» I support _____.

» What is something you can do about it? You can always learn more and become more involved with it. Read about what you support. Volunteer in the organization you support or donate something, small or big. How can actions you take today express love to your family members or friends? Maybe send a text message, or call, or wash dishes, or clean the house, or fix something for them. Something small with an action. Try it.

IMPROMPTU OP. 90, NO. 3
BY FRANZ SCHUBERT

ranz Schubert is one composer whose music I believe I would play differently in every stage of my life. There is a certain quality in his music that I feel calls forth so much more expression, and my interpretation of it changes and grows as I mature. I often say that, if I had the chance to meet up with a composer and chat over coffee, I would choose Schubert. Something about his music, with its range of emotion, atmosphere, and sonority, makes me want to get to know him as a person.

Schubert had a strong group of friends who were called Schubertiads. Apparently, they used to meet two or three times a week to discuss music, poetry, food, dance, games, and gymnastics, while taking excursions into the countryside. Maybe having this strong support system in his life had something to do with his amazing music making. Even though he passed away when he was only thirty-one years old, he composed many volumes of compositions in a relatively short amount of time. When he turned nineteen, he had already composed his third symphony and more than two hundred songs.[7]

---

7   If you'd like to read more about Schubert's life, try *The Life of Schubert* by Christopher H. Gibbs.

An impromptu is a free-form musical composition, which has an improvisational character as if it had been made up on the spot. Just like an insightful thought may come in a moment of intuition, this piece of music, Impromptu Op. 90, No. 3, has very deep meaning, but it was composed in only a matter of minutes—not days or years—despite its richness. If given the choice of only one piece to play as the last concert of my life, I would choose this impromptu by Schubert, without hesitation. It brings me to a place where, after all the struggle is over, hope remains.

There was only one occasion in my pianist career that I cried during my performance. It was not the sobbing variety of crying, but I had teary eyes as I was performing this piece as an encore in one concert. In that particular stage of my life, I was going through a difficult time. Before I performed it, I told everyone in the audience that this piece of music reminds me of the message that everything will be all right, even if I might be in the middle of a great life storm. It always tells me, "Jeeyoon, it is okay. All is well. Stay still." Then after I went through this piece onstage with such emotion, I felt that a seed of hope was planted, for me to gain the strength to start my life again.

I want to give this back to you here.

No words necessary.

Simply receive what this music holds, with an open heart. It will give you the strength you might need today, telling you that everything will be okay.

Please go to my podcast, *Journey Through Classical Piano*, Season 1, Episode 13, to listen.

To listen to the piece and learn more about it, scan here ▶

MOVEMENT #5

Take Care of Your Body and Your Environment

1

THE POWER OF WALKING

When a student has an issue with a certain passage in music, or when I notice they're not practicing effectively, I often ask questions that cover some basics of well-being. Did you sleep well last week? How long did you sleep? What did you eat? Did you move well last week? What did you do? More often than not, when the very basics of movement, sleep, or eating habits are not in the right place, there is a little crack in my students' way of practice, or their mind, or their overall physical health, which inevitably affects the way they play what they've practiced.

For me, this is all connected. The reason I walk is connected to my desire for becoming a better pianist and better person. We are complicated creatures. Maybe we can't measure the effect of our activities numerically, but one thing is for sure: Movement is a must for us, regardless of its form, that serves our mind and body. You may be a bicycler, or a swimmer (as I am), or enjoy doing other kinds of activities, but walking is a basic form of movement and it's easy to get started—no special gear or instruction is necessary. Simply put on comfortable shoes and go outside.

For me, movement—any kind of movement—has helped me find balance in my whole being. It helps me reboot myself daily. Simply because I moved yesterday, it doesn't mean I am okay not to move today. Just like eating meals every day, movement or exercise needs to be a part of my daily lifestyle. Once I figured this secret out myself, many potential problems or issues ended up fixing themselves. It has given me time to separate work and take a break, boosting my emotional well-being, helping my brain attain new information or process existing information, and connecting with myself and with others better. I couldn't remain healthy and functional if I stopped my daily movement.

On the day of a performance, I go for a walk and practice my music in my head. Sometimes weather may not allow me to walk outside, but I always prefer preparing for my concert with my usual walk. On those days, I don't hurry the steps, and I may pause to take in beautiful scenery, but in my head is a slow tempo of the music that I will be playing that night. There is something about walking that helps me calm down, get in touch with myself better, and prepare myself for the concert mentally, emotionally, and physically.

I have always liked to walk. In Korea, it was a normal part of my lifestyle. I had to walk quite some distance to my school or to my piano institute or for a morning hike to a nearby mountain or to a grocery store. All of my regular destinations were reached on foot until I reached high school. There was no picking me up from the school by a car or a school bus. I had to walk there.

> Walking is a humbling activity for me. If I am walking, that means I am healthy, I am alive, and I am here.

I remember those times that I used to daydream or enter into a meditative state with my communal walking. Back then, there was no cell phone, nothing to distract me from simply walking. Sometimes I met up with a friend at the midpoint to school, then we walked together, or my nanny met up with me at the gate of the school and we walked back home with my dog, Jenny. When I look back, lots of great memories took place on the road when I walked. Maybe life itself took place on the road: I laughed, I encountered many great discoveries, I dreamed, and sometimes I cried. Something about the humble activity of walking always has made me appreciate what I have. After all, walking requires nothing more than simply showing up and moving one step in front of the other. If I am walking, that means I am healthy, I am alive, and I am here.

One of the best kinds of days for me always includes a good walk. Nowadays I try to go for a good ten thousand steps each day, which equates to about an hour and twenty minutes. That is my time to day-dream or disconnect or rest or think or simply do the act of moving. I sometimes meet up with friends for a walk. As much time as I spend on the piano bench, I am very aware that it is sedentary and make a con-scious effort to move to counterbalance it. Often, it's difficult for me to distinguish a time for rest and a time for work, as my piano is right there in my house all the time. By including a regular walk in my lifestyle, it punctuates a time to take a break and move away from the piano.

I have tried to rest by simply lying down on a bed or couch as a way to take a break, but for me the only true rest for my mind and body turns out to be through moving. Comparing thirty minutes of sitting down on a couch versus thirty minutes of walking, the latter always leaves me feeling a dramatic difference in my energy level and readiness to start my next activity. I don't lie to myself (as much as I want to sometimes) that just sitting or lying is rest. It can certainly work sometimes, but for the most part, going out for a walk is the best way for me to rest from what I've been doing. I plug in com-pletely, then I unplug completely.

For me, walking represents life's journey. It is not about finishing, but about simply being on the road and in the process. I can always change my pace according to my mood and condition. Slowing down or taking a break from a walk is totally fine and often needed. We push ourselves without taking time to slow it down in life. The key is that I need to be aware of myself. Am I tired? Do I have the energy to push? Do I need to slow down a bit now? How long should my stride be today? It's always empowering to feel my own legs take one step and then another, connecting myself to the earth through my feet. It's easy now, but walking is indeed a complicated movement for our whole body to coordinate. After all, we had to learn how to walk after falling many times when we were babies.

I like the humbleness of this very act that all humans are meant to do. One foot and then the other, one step at a time. No matter

> A break spent walking always gives me a clear distinction between work and rest, both physically and mentally.

what kind of mood I am in before a long walk, without a doubt I always come back with a better one. For me, walking is my super-secret anti-depression pill, giving me the mental boost I need. I feel it each time. I always look forward to that feeling after a walk, which is refreshed and ready to embark on my next thing. I need this movement, so afterward I can perform at maximum efficiency.

There is much scientific research out there on how physical activity helps our emotional well-being. One such report that resonates with me is "runner's high," which takes place not only in running, but also can occur after twenty minutes of other cardiac intensity. I have been experiencing my own version of runner's high every time I walk. If we were in ancient times, we might have been foraging or hunting—which includes walking.

As much as I wish piano were a more primal activity of human nature, I cannot change that aspect about it. Though it does entail some movement, there is nothing like walking as a primitive activity, as the human body was designed to do. As we walk, we feel connected to ourselves, and generate a release of endorphins that is often hidden within us.

Do you have anything on your mind? Do you feel down? Do you want to feel more refreshed? Do you need a break? Do you want to be more creative? Try to go for a long walk or do any kind of movement: dance, swim, bike, hike, or just start moving around the house more. Make a decision to move. Then do it over and over again.

Don't overthink it. The one thing that we all can do right now is walking.

For me, it does wonders.

SOMETHING TO TRY WHENEVER YOU'RE READY:

- Make a plan to walk for at least 20 minutes every day this week and see how you feel.

- Do some physical activity like running, swimming, biking, walking, or hiking as a form of relaxation and a break. Before you do it, always think first about that good feeling you get afterward. For me, it helps to get over the initial laziness or procrastination before any physical activity by thinking about its positive effect on me.

- Try to meet up with your friends for walking rather than at a restaurant or a coffee shop, or call while you walk. I always have a great conversation while I walk.

- Taking it to the next level . . . Try to walk 10,000 steps for a month and see if that affects you positively. (I am very curious to hear the outcome.) When you have the energy, walk at a brisk tempo with longer strides.

2

AWAKEN WITH
MEDITATION

I was looking at a clock in my greenroom before a concert where I would play *Rhapsody in Blue* with the Purdue University Orchestra in Indiana. It was seven o'clock, which meant I could do about fifteen minutes of meditation before I had to go onstage at 7:30. As usual, I set a timer on my phone and started to focus on my breathing, counting from one to ten with each inhale and exhale, and then repeated the process.

A moment later, a stage manager notified me that in fact my part of the program was not until eight p.m. I thought, "Okay, that means I have about forty-five minutes for meditation. That is quite a long time. But I might as well make the best of it." So that is what I did, meditating almost an hour before this concert in my greenroom, as opposed to my usual fifteen minutes. I don't think about specific music right before the performance, nor do I think about the concert. When I went onstage that night, for some very strange reason, it felt as though I had been breathing through an oxygen tank just before then. Life seemed to be like a movie in slow motion; I saw everything with such clarity. There was no fogginess, no mental battle. My mind was amazingly clear, where there was only one thing that existed in the whole world: music. As I played the last note triumphantly next to a full orchestra howling with the final chords, I felt such bliss, maybe a taste of heaven, in that very moment with everything—the music, orchestra, piano, audience, conductor, other musicians, and myself. A thought came into my mind quietly, "Whatever I did to prepare for this concert today, I need to do it again. This is a revelation."

I had been practicing meditation for quite some time until that point, but that was the first time I felt the direct effect of meditation in a very tangible and powerful way on a stage. I thought if I could experience that kind of mental clarity every time I am on a stage, it would be absolutely amazing. With the hope of chasing that level of clarity, I have practiced meditation more seriously since then. For me, meditation is nothing fancy. During ten or fifteen minutes of protected time, I sit down on the floor, close my eyes, and try to focus on everything about that very moment physically, environmentally, and emotionally. I may hear some sounds outside, or my own noise from inside.

> I long for mental clarity onstage and in life. A meditation practice is one of the tools that helps me get closer to that.

Simply by focusing on my breathing, which is happening rhythmically and repeatedly in my body, I feel centered into being in the now, and I become able to recognize some random visits of thoughts or emotions arising during that time. Sometimes visualizing a ray of light moving through my body up and down while I focus on breathing has helped me find focus in the moment. Although I feel I am quite a beginner in this matter, even with seven years of daily practice, I can say that my relationship with meditation is deepening with time.

You may never have to perform in a concert in the way I do, but I am sure you will benefit from the principles of meditation if you are open to it. Imagine having better control of yourself emotionally. Imagine being more at ease and more peaceful, on a daily basis. Imagine being in a closer relationship with yourself, knowing your own thoughts and emotional patterns. Imagine being able to escape from your own head much more easily and perceptively and being able to enjoy each moment of your life more fully. A meditation practice may open that door for you.

I find it interesting that I have not had such an intense feeling after meditation since that evening of the Gershwin concert, even with my consistent practice of meditation. It almost feels like I am chasing that bliss I once experienced as the highest point of possibility onstage in terms of mental clarity. At the same time, I know that concert experience was only possible because of my meditation, so I keep hoping for that state of mind every time I give a concert, preparing with every tool I know is helpful, including meditation. For me, as a performer, the difference between using meditation and not using it is night and day.

The first time I encountered meditation, I was in a difficult time in my life as I struggled with a broken relationship. A friend of mine recommended a meditation app called Headspace. With a hope of finding some relief from my pain, I tried it. I had nothing to lose. In those days, I was counting the hours until I could be alone so I could cry without worrying about having puffy eyes or being seen as an emotional wreck, as I had to pretend to be normal in front of my students. I told myself, "After five p.m., when I finish my work, I can cry. Hold on a couple more hours here."

I discovered that the word "heartbroken" is literally a physical pain, a feeling of pain in my chest. When I first tried the meditation app at home, it didn't seem to work. The emotional pain was still there, and no magic happened. I thought I was just covering up the pain with trying to control my breathing. At times, the voice from the guided meditation app seemed annoying. I said to the phone, "You don't understand! I can't do this!"

But I kept doing it regularly, even with those doubts and annoyances. I don't know why. I think I liked having company in those difficult times—a real voice I could talk back to. One day, after doing that app for two months or so, I realized that I did not have to think about counting the hours until I could cry, nor did I feel pain in my chest during the day. I started to look forward to getting my dose of peace in my quiet moments with meditation, thinking about nothing but breathing and observing my own "monkey mind." That is how I got to know about meditation, and it has become one of my daily tools for life on and off the stage.

I can never say how exactly one tool is impacting my life in any measurable way, but I can say with a meditation practice that I am much quicker to notice my mind than before. Especially against negative thoughts and emotions, this tool has become effective for me. A couple of months ago, I had a feeling, which I'm not sure how to describe in words, that something weird was going on when I was walking down empty aisles in a grocery store due to COVID-19.

> When I suffer an emotional attack in life, my daily practice of meditation shines by helping me remain aware of the unnecessary overreaction. This prevents me from becoming a victim of my own emotions.

There was no food, no toilet paper, no water bottles, basically nothing left in that store. In that very moment, I noticed my mind was going to a dark place. Maybe that was a fear or a worry that the world would come to an end. Realizing this shift in my emotions, I started to focus on my breathing, simply observing my own mind, as my emergency meditation. It helped. I was able to carry on and moved on to the next agenda item that day without being dramatically dragged into a deep hole of negativity.

With meditation, I've learned that I can always direct my focus back to *now*, and I don't have to be caught in the middle of my own emotions or thoughts. I'm able to detach myself from my own thoughts. This was a powerful tool for me. It feels like meditation has served as a pause button for my life whenever I felt bad or low or anxious. It also helped me remove myself from the scene, with the thought that I could always return to it in fifteen minutes. The truth is that, when I went back to that very scene of emotion afterward, it always felt less intense.

When I am on the stage, there are always millions of thoughts coming into and out of my head. These thoughts have nothing to do with my music making in that moment, but at the same time, it is still me—still my thoughts. Being able to detach myself from my own thought process and not getting carried away or being a victim is exactly what I am practicing with daily meditation. More often than not, I find that meditation makes me better able to make changes to my thoughts. It doesn't mean I become less emotional. It simply means that I have a tool to prevent myself from being a victim of emotions and hopefully make myself more at ease. It also teaches me how I can stay present in the moment more effectively. The sounds I hear,

> Being more in the present moment and enjoying every second of it—that is something I practice with meditation.

the food I am eating, the people I am seeing, the voices I hear, the music I am feeling, the touch I feel on a piano. Meditation makes me feel as though I can slow these down in my mind, helping me savor each moment more deeply.

These days I start my group piano classes with two minutes of meditation. Nothing fancy. We focus on our breathing, then we start our music making. My wish is for my students to be more aware of this tool whenever they need it in their own practice or life, understanding that being aware of our own mind is a step to becoming a better musician. In fact, my student Kelly thanked me during our lesson, saying she finally is doing a daily meditation and it's helped her be a better pianist—and surely helped in her recent solo piano recital preparation. She believes that the improvement she felt from her last piano performance was largely due to her daily meditation practice for a month prior. She'd known about this tool for years, but she was finally ready to try.

I find that playing the piano is very meditative by nature, as I can also observe my mind while I play. But what is different in playing piano compared to pure meditation is that when I play, my mind is busy following the music and staying *in* the music. On the other hand, during a meditation practice, I intentionally direct my mind to go either to my breathing or to a specific sensation. One of my favorite moments in my daily meditation is that toward the end for a minute or so, I let my mind do whatever it wants. It is a fun and helpful discovery for me to learn more about myself by following where my mind goes when it is completely loose.

There is a book about meditation called *10% Happier*. I like the fact that the title is not overly promising. I agree with it. Meditation may not be one solution for everything, but maybe it can help. For now, I just want to remind you that it's there, whenever you are curious or ready to try. For me, this meditation tool helped me be a better person and a better pianist, having a tool to handle my emotions and learning to be more awake in my life. Like everything, this tool takes practice. Maybe years, more likely a lifetime. But that is a direction I would like to go. A place where I can be more content, more awake, more peaceful, and more settled in the now. I hope you consider joining me.

SOMETHING TO TRY
WHENEVER YOU'RE READY:

- Meditation is nothing fancy. Simply put a timer on for 3 minutes now and start counting your breaths. Breathe in for one, breathe out for two. When you reach ten, then start back again with one. The key is to gather your mind to focus on your breathing. Some thoughts might take you other places, but don't go there. Observe it as if it is someone else's thought. Watch your thoughts arising and going while you feel and focus on your body breathing in and out. Be with it.

- My favorite three apps for guided meditations are Calm, Headspace, and Waking Up. I still like to do a guided meditation regularly, although I can certainly do it solo. It is simply a preference. Sometimes you like to walk alone, other times you don't mind having company walking along with you.

- While you are stuck in traffic or in a grocery line, try to meditate by focusing on your breathing. It is a perfect excuse to be with yourself.

3

GET IN TOUCH
WITH YOUR BODY
THROUGH YOGA

A week after a concert, I often do lots of resting poses in yoga to calm me down. As much as it is exciting and rewarding to give a concert, I always find that it's difficult for me to come down to earth, and I feel almost depressed. Maybe it's similar to postpartum depression. After such an intense and climactic event, your mind and body need an adjustment to come back to normal.

There is a tremendous amount of preparation and buildup for any concert, requiring me to have laser-sharp focus. I find that as much as I need to be my best self to be able to share music and give a concert in public, I also need to find myself back in the simple life of being just another human, Jeeyoon. People might think it would be harder to prepare for a concert than to prepare for afterward. For me, however, I often have more difficulty sleeping in the days after a concert, as I keep playing back the music in my head and have a hard time turning it off. It requires almost an equal amount of work to come down from the top of the mountain. When all the shining lights of the concert and crowds disappear, starting another normal day with a simple breakfast requires an adjustment, as I still feel a rush of adrenaline lingering in my body.

I find that yoga is extremely helpful for me in these periods. It teaches me a lesson of letting go. I always wish my good memories from a concert would last longer and my bad memories would disappear as quickly as possible. Regardless of my wishes, I have learned that the feeling passes. Even with the most amazing concerts, it passes. Even with horrible failures or challenges, it still passes. All I can do in these passing events in life is to be grounded with myself and my body. I am certainly not a pro at it, but I am trying. I can't imagine a preparation or a finish to my day—especially a concert day—without yoga. It centers me into a peaceful place that makes me content and grounded.

Have you ever worked really hard toward something, then when it is over it seems difficult to get back to your normal life? A principle of yoga is to center our body and inevitably end up centering our mind, which follows the body. When you have a hard time directing your mind in a certain way, an answer might lie in the way you are holding or moving your body. Often, we hold our stress, frustration, and anxiety in a certain part of the body, maybe in your jaw, maybe in your shoulder, or in your hip. By opening up the body with a yoga practice, the mind follows, as our negative emotions find release. After all, mind and body reside in the same place—in you. You may not have experienced yoga or not find it of interest, but you can always learn from the principles of yoga, which is to accept what is, be gentle with yourself, and learn to let go.

I signed up for a Korean martial art, tae kwon do, when I was thirteen. Maybe I had watched too many Chinese martial arts movies during that time, but I thought it would be fun to be able to become a pianist who was also a skilled kung fu girl who could protect herself from danger. I dreamed about doing those swift movements and kicks that I'd seen in movies. On my first day, the only thing my teacher asked me to do was stretch my legs. For the following week, that was still the only thing I had to do—stretch my legs more. It was painful and I saw no noticeable progress. I quickly realized that I was severely inflexible and learned that in tae kwon do, being able to open your legs to almost 180 degrees was the basic move. That was the first step I needed to do before learning any skills in tae kwon do. I didn't last more than two weeks, unfortunately, but I was relieved that I didn't have to force myself to stretch my inflexible legs. I have continued to focus on my finger movements and stretches on piano, but I gave up the notion of becoming a kung fu pianist. I avoided any kind of leg stretching after that.

A friend of mine mentioned casually over lunch that she was taking a yoga lesson.

I said, "Yoga? It is just a full hour of stretching. It sounds painful. Is that a group class at the YMCA?"

"No," she said, "it is a private class. I meet with this incredible yogi who is a former ballet dancer from NYC once a week for a lesson. It is absolutely amazing."

Until then, my notion about yoga was just a lazy version of working out with very painful stretching; I always assumed that when people said they did some yoga "workout," it was their way of avoiding a real workout. I preferred sweating and doing hard workouts, and it seemed inefficient to spend an hour doing some movement without getting any feeling of having done a lot of work. I also thought yoga was something that was always done in a group. I never knew it could be a private lesson. In that time, coincidently, I'd just finished reading the book *Younger Next Year*, where the author raved about his yoga practice. I became curious about yoga in that moment—maybe there was something more to it that I didn't know.

So, I followed my curiosity and called that instructor for an appointment. For some reason, her mellow Zen voice instantly calmed my body. We met for the first time that week for a private session. That is how I started my yoga practice about three years ago. I still meet with my teacher once a week and practice on my own regularly. The more I understand yoga, the more I feel that need to learn more about it. It feels very similar to my journey of piano; it is

> Once I understood the essence of yoga, I was hooked. It was similar to my journey with piano. It is about the process.

not about going to the finish line, but is a process of creating in the moment. I finally let yoga come into my life properly to take me on that journey.

In one of the interviews I had in the past, I was asked, "If you could go back in time ten years, what would you like to tell yourself?"

I answered, "Jeeyoon, start doing yoga now."

Perhaps you think of yoga as some kind of current trend enjoyed mostly by women. Allow me to remind you that the development of yoga can be traced back more than five thousand years. It has a long rich history that has proven to help humankind.

In India, when you go see a doctor, you may be prescribed with yoga poses, depending on your symptoms. If you have indigestion, you might be asked to do some forward bending or twisting movements. If you have depression, you might be asked to do lots of grounding positions like a warrior pose or a certain pose bending your back. You will need to practice these poses every day for months. When yogis wake up in the morning, they start with a pose like downward-facing dog, which is basically a pose with your hands and feet spread apart on the ground in an inverted-V shape. That kind of basic pose teaches the yogis which specific body part that day needs more attention, and they then practice accordingly. I find that this kind of awareness of one's body is fascinating. I always wanted to learn more about my own mind, but I never had a similar awareness with my own body. The more I practiced yoga, the more I grew to desire an awareness of my body, which is inevitably connected to my mind. My mind rests in my body; my body rests in my mind. They became one in yoga.

"Jeeyoon, let it go."

My yogi master, Bernadette, was gently pushing my back when I was doing a pigeon pose, which stretches the hip flexor. It is interesting how each hip is different from the other and has its own personality. When I let go slightly in the place where I was gripping too hard—a subtle thing that most people won't notice—something shifted dramatically within my mind. That small space made my body become one inch taller, or so it felt. I also learned that each pose has a certain effect, such as a standing pose called "warrior," which helps me feel more grounded, confident, and ready to charge into the world. I have several poses I rely on to prepare myself in the greenroom right before my concerts. These include those standing poses. An open chest, wide and tall hands, and grounding legs give the signal to my body and to my mind that I am getting ready to be in charge of my performance, which in turn gives me a strong, empowering energy. Since I don't have to carry my own instrument, the only thing I need to bring for my concert is my performance dress, shoes, and a yoga mat.

Nowadays, when I wake up, I am able to diagnose or prescribe myself a certain move in yoga. "Today, my lower back is acting up, I should do a, b, and c. I feel anxious, I should do x, y, and z. My hamstrings are tight, I should do this pose a bit longer." These inner dialogues carry me into my day. I often give myself a certain move as a gift to myself. "You deserve ten minutes of a resting pose right now." That sweet movement leaves me with a rewarding sense of peace.

For me, yoga is a way of life, not just another workout or a new trend. I love having a quiet conversation with myself through the movements in yoga, learning to be gentle with myself as my own healer. I find that it can be difficult for me to be kind to myself. In practicing yoga, I can remind myself each day to accept what is. I am amazed at how important yoga has become to me, and how these movements teach me life lessons, being able to connect better with myself and the universe. Yoga is a moving meditation, as movement is simply a way for us to keep breathing and being aware of breathing. When I finish a good yoga session, the effect feels similar to that of meditation, and my body feels rejuvenated.

> With yoga, I am learning to be one step closer to being able to "let go" and accept life as it is.

The difference compared to pure meditation is that in yoga, I let my body become the leader of my mind; the body goes first and the mind follows. I am still inflexible like before, but I meet my inflexible self with a gentleness, asking if there is any room for more opening up. Maybe one day, as my body loosens up more, my mind will be able to follow that space to be more peaceful and spacious.

I highly recommend you try out yoga, in any shape or form. When you finally understand the essence of it, then try to discover it even deeper. Just like going up a mountain, simply climbing straight up and down isn't the same as if you slow down, try out new trails, and discover more each day. The journey will reward you with more discovery about yourself, your body, your mind, and peace.

SOMETHING TO TRY
WHENEVER YOU'RE READY:

- Any ache or pain in your body today? Try to find that specific ache-focused yoga on YouTube now and try it for 10 minutes. For example, yoga for low back pain or yoga for a tight hamstring.

- What are you feeling now? Try to find that feeling-related yoga practice on YouTube. For example, yoga for depression or morning coffee cup flow for boosting energy.

- Try to find a private instructor. For me, this was a game changer to really learn deeply about yoga at my own pace in my own body. Just like taking a piano lesson, a good instructor will be able to guide you on this fascinating journey of yoga and help you discover more about yourself and life.

4

YOU ARE WHAT YOU EAT

I always think about what I plan to eat on concert days well in advance. I like to experiment with how what I eat during the day affects me physically and mentally, then try to apply it during real performance days. Over the years, I've learned that foods affect my performance much more significantly than I once thought. Certain kinds of food make it easier to focus than others during an entire concert, and I sometimes notice a subtle change in my energy level.

Often giving a concert feels like running a marathon, requiring every ounce of energy from myself. I don't eat anything heavy right before a concert, as I learned this makes my body work harder to digest foods than to do the other important work of playing piano with a clear mind. Heavy foods make me feel tired or sleepy. I have also wondered, "What about the other days, when I don't perform? Don't I need to

> What we eat affects our mind. That is one of the important reasons that I am very conscious about what I eat.

treat myself well then, too?" Although I am not an athlete who might have a nutrition expert on-site as part of my training, I believe that what I eat significantly affects me as a pianist and a person.

There is no one-size-fits-all solution for nutrition. We have physical, environmental, and cultural differences. Plus, we have strong preferences for what we like to eat and what we believe is good for us. I don't believe that what works for me will automatically work for others. We need to custom design our unique nutritional system by simply experimenting on ourselves. I believe that it is important for us to become educated about nutrients and foods in general and try to be open minded about experimenting with foods we might not be interested in, such as eating more vegetables. We can always make a conscious choice about what we believe is good for our body and mind. Body, mind, and soul are connected, and what we eat shapes significantly how our day goes and how prepared we are to perform on our stage of life.

Many musicians have heard at some point in their lives that eating bananas is a magic solution for performance nerves. Some may swear by it, and others just don't think it's true. I do eat bananas sometimes before a performance, not because I believe that it helps for performance nerves, but for me it is a simple and easy food that doesn't require much energy for my body to digest. I know that bananas can be digested within two hours, which is great timing before a concert.

It has been almost four years since I started experimenting with not eating red meat, and then a few months later I eliminated chicken from my diet. A few months after that, I got rid of any dairy products in my diet. It was a gradual, step-by-step experiment. I enjoy going to my favorite sushi restaurant every now and then, but other than that, I don't eat much fish. I started to experiment with my diet out of curiosity about how certain foods affected my performance—in mind and body. I already had a diet with lots of fruits and vegetables from my upbringing, so saying a complete no to meat and dairy was an easy call for me.

But when I started referring to myself as a vegan, I got all kinds of different reactions. Some friends asked when or if I would go back to eating "normal" foods, the way I used to eat. Some wanted to educate me about the importance of vitamin B1 or iron from meats; others thought I was being picky, worried my life would be boring without a variety of foods. But many friends accepted

> Do you know how certain kinds of foods affect you differently? Do you know what is good for you? Start experimenting.

my choice without comment or judgment. Although initially I found myself explaining why I had decided to experiment in the first place, I gradually stopped. I accept that what others think or say does not have any impact on me, as it's not about their bodies, but about my own.

What I have been doing with my experiment is not only saying no to meat and dairy, but also eating less processed foods, less sugar, and more whole foods. I always preferred being able to recognize food in its original shape and taste. I mostly eat seasonal fruits at breakfast, and I stopped drinking coffee. Drinking coffee made me too jittery in live performances. Skipping coffee only on performance days was more difficult, so I eventually decided to stop drinking coffee altogether, which also helped my night sleep by helping me feel naturally tired at the end of the day.

I thought experimenting with my diet would be difficult, but I am surprised by how easy and fun it was—and natural. I feel as though I have been eating this way for my whole life. I have become more and more addicted to feeling good and having more energy throughout the day. Then, something very interesting took place during my first year since the initial experiment: I desired fewer fancy meals in general, being happier with simple foods. As much of a foodie as I am, this was very unexpected. This made me think I could be totally content with simple foods for the rest of my life. No fancy decoration needed! Juicy sweet corn from the farmers' market and a delicious watermelon on a summer day made me happier than an elaborate meal. My palate has come to desire healthy, clean, simple, unadorned, and less-cooked foods. When foods are produced naturally and organically, they always taste sweeter and truer—as they should. Farmers' markets have been a great place for me to get those kinds of locally produced vegetables and seasonal fruits.

The real change that was the most dramatic for me was mental. Overall, I was feeling less emotionally drained. My lows were less low than before, feeling more stable in general and more peaceful. I think about Korean Buddhist monks being vegan, and their peaceful dispositions. Maybe that has something to do with it. I am not sure. All I know is that it works for me, too. I felt like I went from feeling like a wild tiger to a peaceful deer, simply by changing my diet. Maybe I am overstating this, or putting too much emphasis on food, as I am sure other aspects of my life have contributed positively to this shift. But that is exactly how I feel.

> I learned how to be totally content with simple foods. That was one unexpected outcome from my experiments.

In the course of the experiment with my diet, I also learned that we have two kinds of modes in our body: when it's digesting food, and when it's not. The stomach, which is the pickiest among all other organs for digestion, has a system like a laundry machine. When there is food inside, the machine starts working. When another new food comes into the system before the previous food is not all the way digested, then instead of putting the cleaner ones out first, the stomach ends up mixing them all up, and starts the process again until there is nothing left to digest. The timing varies depending on the food, but it takes about three to five hours to digest food in the stomach, regardless of the amount of activity afterward. That means the foods that are relatively ready to go to the next organ end up staying in the stomach unnecessarily longer if you keep adding new foods, especially when you eat the wrong foods together, every hour or two. As a result, undigested food is left in your stomach and it rots or ferments, which can cause illness or weight gain.

This was interesting for me to learn. Eating too often or eating a less-than-ideal combination of food types, like combining slow-processing foods with faster ones, such as eating fatty foods along with fresh fruits, makes our stomach work constantly—often for hours. This is not necessary.

Behind the scenes, our body is constantly working without our realizing it. Digesting foods is a lot of work for the body to complete each day. With this notion in mind, I realized that I could make it easier for my body, especially when I focused on important work such as playing piano at a concert. When I know my body doesn't have to

> When I need to focus on my performance, I don't want my body to work too hard to digest foods.

work too hard to digest, I feel more clear. I always give my body time to digest beforehand, eating foods in moderation before a performance.

When I eat also became an interesting experiment. Fasting is a fascinating concept, which many nutrition experts and doctors have proven to provide mental and physical benefits. Although I've never tried to fast for more than a day, I do regularly practice intermittent fasting by giving my body proper time to rest. This involves basically not eating for twelve to sixteen hours each day. For example, if I finish eating at seven p.m., I would not eat anything until the next morning at eight or nine a.m. Finishing eating four to five hours before you sleep is a simple rule. Digestion really slows down and can lead to heartburn or acid reflux in our throats. I certainly hate the experience of waking up in the morning after going to bed without allowing my body to digest. I always feel groggy and get puffy eyes. This way of giving time for the body to rest makes it possible to maximize the efficiency of its function rather than overworking it all the time. When I end up eating too much or too often, I notice that I am tired and become sleepy, even during the day. I am sure you have experienced this also. This feeling is basically our body telling us that it's working too hard, giving us the hint that it is overloaded.

Our stomach doesn't work while we sleep. Don't give it work to do when it's time to sleep. A solid 3 to 4 hours of time is needed for the stomach to digest all its food

---

I've rarely met anyone who doesn't have any weak spot in their food consumption. I also have struggles with what I shouldn't be eating, or not eating in moderation, or those guilty-pleasure foods that I seek (such as freshly baked croissants, dark chocolate, Korean street foods like *duk bok gi*, Korean rice cakes, ramen, and so on). My simple rule for foods is that eighty percent of what I consume should be very healthy, with twenty percent wiggle room. If I am eating mostly healthy, then my body allows me to eat some less-healthy options, as long as the ratio is reasonable. Once I defined myself as a healthy person, the decision I make for each day became easier by simply asking myself, "What would a healthy person choose?" By creating that motto representing the person that I *want* to be, I can more easily answer, "I *don't* eat unhealthy foods," rather than "I *can't* eat unhealthy foods."

I no longer long for a bad bunch of seemingly "tasty" foods of the variety that I used to enjoy. This does not take willpower, but simply remembering that I like to feel good in my body all of the time, have extra energy without any chronic problems, and, more importantly, exist clearheadedly. My taste buds have evolved to where healthy foods taste the best, and I want nothing else.

All these experiments that I have been doing with myself illustrate my own unique journey to finding balance and joy, maintaining a healthy mind and body for what I would like to do in life. What I've learned is that the more sensitive I am to the subtle cues my body sends me regarding food, the more I want to help my body perform its best by giving it what it likes.

I wonder if you know what works for you. Not your food preference for taste, but what kinds of foods work the best for your maximum efficiency of performance. I wonder if you're conscious about the time of day when you eat, and how that affects your performance—such as not eating at night before you sleep. I wonder if you've ever eliminated certain foods to see how you feel, not because it's a new trend or others suggest it, but because you seek the best custom-designed diet to nourish you. Have you tried adding or removing certain food groups from your diet to see how this makes you feel?

> As long as you are eating healthy most of the time, I find it is okay to let yourself stray at times. Always ask, "What would a healthy person choose?"

I'm not the only one with a "stage" to perform on. You have your own *life* stage to perform on each day. What should you eat for the best possible performance each day? Experiment with this concept, and listen to your body. If you seem to find a way that works best for you, then try to eat that way more often than not. Don't stop experimenting, but keep learning about your body in your own way. Nobody else can do it for you. You're the expert when it comes to your own body. Start that journey with yourself now!

SOMETHING TO TRY
WHENEVER YOU'RE READY:

- Write down what you eat this week and record how you feel after each meal and in general over the course of the day. Take a look at the list and see if there is any relation between what you eat and how you feel.

- Before trying to add anything healthy to your diet, first consider eliminating one bad item.

- Eliminate a certain type of food—dairy, processed foods, and so on—for a month and see how you feel.

- Try not to eat anything for at least 3 to 4 hours before you sleep. Make that your life habit.

- Imagine that you have an important event such as public speaking or anything requiring your best performance. What do you choose to eat that day? Can you repeat that on another day?

- Notice any signals that the body is sending, such as sleepiness or feeling tired after eating certain foods. That may mean you ate too much, more than your body can process easily, or perhaps not an optimal combination of foods.

- Eat less sugary foods—for your mind and body.

- Eat more seasonal foods.

5

DESIGN YOUR ENVIRONMENT FOR YOURSELF

I've always wished that I could carry my own instrument. Violinists and flutists who can carry their instruments in such a compact way cannot understand the unique struggle I feel as a pianist, encountering a new, foreign instrument on every stage, with limited time to get to know it prior to a concert. More often than not, a piano that I need to perform on in less than five hours may have some issues that I don't expect: The sound in the high register is too muted, or the pedal squeaks, or it has a heavy key action, or it produces an uneven tone. Even though those pianos onstage might look fabulous, the unique personality of each piano is something every pianist has to adjust to every time we play on them.

There were a couple of occasions where I almost wanted to cancel the concert, as the piano was not in a "workable" condition, but I never did because I still believe that it's my job to create beauty out of whatever piano I have in front of me. One of my piano technician friends told me that the real job of being a pianist is to make a bad piano sound good. This made me laugh. Yet there is so much truth in that joke. Sometimes I feel like I've become a magician who gets an out-of-shape piano to sing in a way it never has before.

Meeting each piano for a concert is very much like meeting a person. I need to find out what personality and tendencies each piano has as I begin a conversation in music. The pressure I feel is that I need to figure this out fast, within a couple of hours, before our live conversation goes on display in front of the public. The quickest way for me to break the ice for this raw conversation with each piano (before a concert and even during the concert) is to believe and imagine that

> We always have a relationship with things in our environment. Talk to them and say thank you.

each piano is the most amazing concert grand piano I've ever experienced. The more I ask it to provide colors and tones, without doubting its capacity in my head, the more positive responses I can receive, even from those pianos that seem to have many underlying health conditions. I often receive this feedback from audiences: "I've never heard that piano sound like that. What did you do?"

A piano is obviously a thing made out of wood, and not a living organism. For me, however, a piano has been a living creature for my whole life. I talk, sing, connect, heal, communicate, and express with a piano. Next to the piano in my house, where I practice daily, I keep a journal. Whenever I notice its subtle voice shift or make the slightest change, I write it down and talk to it.

"How are you doing today? You seem a bit unstable today. How can I help you sound better?"

"You are very sensitive today. That is great! Let's talk more."

I may look like a crazy person talking to an inanimate object, but for me a piano does respond when we talk in music. This is where I apply the value of a relationship with things in life. Author and minimalist Marie Kondo advocates the concept of maintaining a joyful life by keeping only things that spark joy. I believe in this principle—that our environment affects our mind in a significant way. Marie asks herself if each and every object in a house "sparks joy." If it does, then she keeps it. If it doesn't, then she touches that thing again and says, "Thank you for serving me in my life thus far. I appreciated having you to make my life easier. Now I will let you go with a smile."

We all have boxes that we have not opened for years, things we haven't used for years, and things we don't currently use but we're hanging on to them in case we need them sometime in the future. We must accept that these things are basically collecting dust in our space and in our mind. If we consider things not as mere objects but as real relationships we value, this connection to them helps us live in more meaningful ways, learning to appreciate things more. Say thank you to your pillow for helping you get a good night's sleep or say thank you to your coat for keeping you warm, or notice that fuzzy happy feeling with your favorite cup that you drink coffee from each morning.

If I can't tell something thank you, or, as Marie said, feel a spark of joy from it, it could well mean that it is time to let it go. Be surrounded only by things that you care about and feel grateful for. This simplifying lifestyle principle has much to teach me in terms of how to live my life joyfully. We are indeed living in a world where we desire things not out of real need, but for a quick fix of "needing" more and more. But by having a deeper relationship with what you already have, and feeling an appreciation for it, I find that it is easier to recognize if this is a need or want. Having a relationship with things in my environment helps me recognize this distinction more easily, so I can make a more conscious choice.

Designing your environment requires daily maintenance and a good screening and storage system. I love the idea of having some system in life that helps me sustain this maintenance by having a default place for each item to go, such as where to put a wallet or keys. After each usage, it simply goes back to its home. I make my bed each morning. This simple daily act is something I choose to do to feel good when I go to bed at night, or during the day when I pass the bed. It makes a world of difference for my mind to go to a bed that is made up, rather than messy. Just like the feeling of being refreshed and renewed after a big spring cleaning, I love feeling joy and the empowerment that comes from putting things back in their original place and having a clean and simple space in my environment.

What I am most fascinated about is the way this simpler environment principle reveals that having fewer things allows our mind to be more creative and encourages new inspiration. Steve Jobs only wore the same kinds of jeans and T-shirts for years in order to simplify his life with fewer choices, leaving more space in his mind for creative thoughts. Although I don't think I would ever wear the same outfits every day as he did, I believe in the principle: Having a simple environment contributes to the optimal performance of our minds. It doesn't have to be anything fancy, but clean and simple.

> Our surroundings affect our minds much more significantly than we think. Design them for your mind to perform at its best.

I try this minimal concept in the most important space in the house: where my piano is located. When I walk into my living room, there is nothing but a piano. No huge couch, dinner table, chairs, coffee table, lamps, or other usual things we'd find in the living room of a typical house; for me, there is only a piano. I have folding chairs that I keep in a closet and use them to turn this space into a little salon for a private concert gathering. Other than that, it is an open and empty space. This way of using my main space has reinforced my sole focus in life, the piano. When I wake up and walk to the living room, my stage of life is right there, without any distractions or clutter in my vision or in my mind. Although there are still ways for me to become truly minimalistic, I try my best to keep things simple. If I have two of something, I give one away. If a thing doesn't serve me anymore, I believe that its term with me might be done, learning to let it go without thinking too much of keeping it "just in case." Those just-in-case scenarios never come, or are too infrequent to justify keeping it in my place to collect dust in my mind. When I have a simple, spacious environment, I notice there is more room for new ideas in my head, and I receive more positive energy from the universe.

Is there anything you want to focus on more in your life? Do you feel low right now? Try to declutter your surroundings. Open your windows and start getting rid of things that you haven't used for years, keeping only the items that make you content and excited. Then mop the floor and clean your room. You may be surprised at how many new ideas arise, or just how renewed you feel as you start your day, simply by cleaning your environment and applying some minimalistic principles in your surroundings. It's all about appreciating things that spark joy in your life, designing your own space for your optimal mind status. In one video, when Marie Kondo enters someone's house, she kneels down on the floor

> A simple environment allows us to be more creative and have more space for thinking.

and thanks the house for providing a roof for the family and protecting them from the outside elements. It was a beautiful and humble ceremony. Just as I talk to a piano as if it is a living organism that I wish to connect with, we can all try to create a special connection with things in our environment.

Keep only those things that make you feel excited and joyful, and design a simple environment for your mind to rest, create, and focus.

SOMETHING TO TRY
WHENEVER YOU'RE READY:

- What is important to you? What is the focus in your life? If there isn't only one, identify a few things in your life.

  1. _____

  2. _____

  3. _____

- Then design your environment based on that notion. Make it your focus to stand out and declutter things that may hinder you from focusing on those things that are most important to you.

- Let's choose one corner of your space and start to clean today. Get rid of things that you haven't used for years and rearrange some of those items again in the way that you can easily scan all of the items that you own. Just like Marie Kondo says, if that object still sparks joy, keep it; and if it doesn't, say thank you and let it go. Don't think too long. I find that a quick, intuitive decision about a thing works for me. (And it always improves with practice.)

- Choose one object that you use today and try to have some conversation either out loud or internally. What can you tell it? What do you like about it, and what are you thankful for?

- Try to build a habit of putting a thing back in its original place. Create a home base for every single item in your house if they don't have one. Hopefully, things piled up on a kitchen countertop are not in their permanent homes! As long as you know where their home should be, put them there after each use. For example, I have a basket that I simply throw my pajamas or clothes that are not quite dirty enough yet for the laundry, but otherwise might wind up on the floor. And I have a little cup at the entrance of the house where I put my keys and other small objects.

- Clean your space now. A neat and organized space might give you a great energy boost and inspiration to start something new.

- Try to make the bed each morning for a month. Experiment with it and see if that works for you positively.

6

THE BEAUTY
OF OUR LIMITS

*B*efore I walk onto a stage, I always think the very concert I am about to give is my last concert. If this is my last concert, what's there to worry about? This way of thinking always liberates me to appreciate the very opportunity that I've been given to share music and sets my mind to give everything I have with no regrets. I always want to walk off the stage feeling that there is absolutely nothing more I could have given in this concert. It was my truly best effort to connect, to enjoy, to feel, to express, and to exist in this very moment fully.

The thing is, that very concert could well be my last concert. We never know when the last day of our lives will come. We didn't decide when to enter this earth, and at the same time we don't get to decide when we leave. I had a milestone fortieth birthday in 2020. In many ways, I feel I am just the same four-year-old girl who used to walk to the piano institute in my little town in Korea. I am surprised at how these forty years have gone by so quickly, and how I don't feel like I am the age

I am. When I was a teenager, I thought forty seemed much older than I feel now. That means that I might feel similarly when I am ninety. Life will go very quickly, as it has done, and my soul within that body will still feel young and fresh. Since I don't know when my last day will arrive, I would like to live my life today as if it is the last day. Life is short, life is sweet, and life is worth living, even with the painful challenges it throws our way.

I loved my dog, Jenny, when I was growing up. She was a little poodle and I had many precious memories with her—going to the park, sleeping with her in my bed, playing outside, walking, and swimming in the ocean. She was my best friend in my youth, and we did everything together. She loved my piano playing also, keeping me company while I practiced.

One day, when I was out in the yard with her to play with the jump rope, she ran toward a car that was approaching us. As the car was coming slowly, I thought things would be okay, thinking the car or Jenny would stop in time. I still ran toward her to grab her leash. Then she thought it was some kind of a tag game, starting to run faster away from me. My heart pounded. "Don't do it, Jenny! Don't!" Then that moment, she disappeared into the front of the car but did not come out the back. I stopped in the middle of the road, not sure how to think or what to do. When I slowly walked toward the car that stopped abruptly and looked underneath it, there was Jenny looking at me. A huge feeling of relief washed over me as I reached my arm under the car and grabbed her little body in my arms. "Oh, you worried me, Jenny." But her body was not resisting back the way she usually would, but simply draped limply in my arms. I looked at her, and my whole world just turned upside down. She was dead.

I have a secret to confess. I've never had another dog since then,

> Walk through each day as if it is the last day of your life. For me, this helps me exist fully in the moment.

not because I don't love them. In fact, I am such an animal lover. But I am afraid of that pain. As much as I value that connection and love despite the pain, I can't dare to have another Jenny and go through that pain again.

I have another confession to make. I am afraid of losing my loved ones, my mom and my dear friends, who are always there for me. I fear what life would be like without their love and support. I feel a pain in my chest even thinking about it. However, I have to choose to live my days without that fear stopping me from functioning in a way I should. I don't irrationally jump on a plane if I want to see my mom in person in Korea, nor do I call a friend as if I am afraid they might be gone tomorrow. I know that I need to keep living with that expected pain, appreciating each one of them fully in my heart. That pain is a part of life that I am afraid to go through, yet it's so meaningful and precious to have these amazing people in my life to love. It is surely worth the pain to have them in my life. Maybe one day, I will be able to have another pet.

I have lost many friends, mentors, and family members in my life, as you probably have also. Every loss has hit me in such a way that I was no longer the same person. The pain of a loss always molded me into someone new. I never got over the loss, but had to learn to live with it. I don't have anything to offer in this matter about how to be stronger or how to deal with it. I am just another fellow human being who also suffers from loss, and from feeling vulnerable and weak.

One thing that has helped me is that I feel the existence of the deceased residing in me as strongly as it did when they lived. They are right there in my head, or in my heart, everywhere I go, living the whole time within me. I still feel the existence of my dog, Jenny, in my heart.

I actually don't think I am afraid of my own death. At least in my head, I'm not, even if I die today. But I do have a wish for my life. That is to live until the last day with a full intention—even with a deteriorating body. As long as I am breathing, I would like to choose to live, to enjoy, to explore, to be curious, to be flexible, to accept, to be positive, to connect, to express, to love, to play, to laugh, and to feel. I don't have the perspective of someone who is ninety, but I am determined with my forty-year-old body and mind that I don't want to give up striving to be a better human being. During that final moment, on my last day, when I feel that my final breath is approaching, I hope I can let go completely, smiling and thinking, "It was a beautiful journey."

There is a Japanese tradition, on each New Year's Day, where people write a poem that would be recited during their imaginary funeral. It is just another way of reminding us of our mortality, realizing it is not forever. I find that it is a beautiful way to ponder this truth at least once a year. Even though we wish we could be here forever, it is true that we have a limited time on this earth, which makes our being here more beautiful and worthwhile. I do believe that our being doesn't disappear after our death, but simply moves to another place. Death then opens another door to the next realm.

> I wish to choose to be curious, to learn, to be flexible, to be positive, to love, to connect, and to feel fully until the last day of my life.

Even though I believe that there is another wonderful place waiting for me after my death, I still wish to create my piece of heaven *now*. A life is worth living now and a life is worth living after. There is no distinction for me. However, since I don't have any perspective of what it will be like after my death or any possibility to come back here to tell you how it is after I die, I choose to do my best in this chapter of my being on this earth, and worry about another when it comes. I can only choose how I live my life today and now. If I want to create a piece of heaven now, I can certainly do it with my intention. I can always choose to connect, to do good and help others, to enjoy, to feel, to be positive and happy, to love, and to do the very thing I love to do, which right now is playing piano. I can choose how to live today fully in my performance of life. If I can do my today well, there is a chance that I am doing my life well. The truth is, we get to experience every day only once. There is no going back, no stopping. In every minute of every unique stage of our lives, we have a choice—to live it fully or waste the precious moment.

> You have a choice, to live fully now or to waste it. If you can do well today, it may mean you are doing your life well.

The stage manager holds the concert stage door and says to me, "I will open this door for you whenever you're ready." When I nod softly and make that decision to walk through the door, there is a beautiful stage opening up to me.

Now, I am behind the stage, holding this door to the performance of your life. It is never too late. Today is another chance that you can make it better. There are no regrets. You are beautiful just the way you are.

Go and play your tune.

All I have shared with you in this book is here to keep you company as a fellow human being in this beautiful concert of yours called a life.

Take a deep breath and choose to walk toward that stage with a big smile,

whenever you're ready.

SOMETHING TO TRY
WHENEVER YOU'RE READY:

Write a short poem for your imaginary funeral just like in that Japanese tradition. And live today as if it is your last day, and appreciate every moment of your life as a gift. Then repeat the process every day. Life is beautiful, isn't it? Here I would like to share my poem with you.

I walked onto a stage with a smile
a velvety tone of a piano
gliding through
a ray of golden sunshine touching our souls

you asked me, was it lonely,
was it hard?

the most beautiful thing often doesn't come easily

what a journey
to be,
and once to have existed
to fill your heart with the magic of music

carry it on
feel it
now go and play your tune.

ENCORE

I love the moment when I play the last note in the program. The excitement from the entire concert has built up to that final moment. I feel relieved, happy, joyful, yet almost sad to finish, hearing the crowd applauding and cheering. Then, for the first time during my entire concert, I disappear backstage.

I still hear thunderous applause and feel the mutual wish to have just one more chance to make a connection. I walk out to the stage again, nod to the audience with a smile, then sit down at the piano to play an encore.

It was such a magical journey for me to write this book for you. If a concert is about becoming a tour guide for a piece of music, this book has been about being a tour guide to my thoughts and the greenroom for my life. Students of mine often say they don't feel comfortable calling themselves pianists, regardless of their levels. I always argue back, saying the definition of pianist is simply someone who plays piano and loves playing piano. I encourage them to call themselves pianists, as they possess everything the definition includes.

I find that it is almost impossible for me to call myself an author, even after writing this book, and it helps me finally understand my students' struggles. I immensely enjoyed communicating with you in words, composing a written concert for you that may help you in your life by hearing how I prepare for my life, and hopefully enticing you to take a step closer to the beauty of classical music.

I wish to continue this conversation with you. While I had a great time taking this journey with you, I still haven't met you! Luckily, I am easily found on the internet. To listen to my music, my albums are available for download or purchase from Amazon or directly from my website. You can always listen to me on my podcast, *Journey Through Classical Piano*, where I post an in-depth session about one classical piece of music. Or you can watch me on my YouTube channel, where I share behind-the-scenes details of being a pianist, as well as some formal and informal live performances.

If you enjoyed this book, you might like to be part of my bi-weekly newsletter, in which I share the thoughts and insights that resonate with me. Please visit my website at www.JeeyoonKim.com and sign up for the newsletter. To share your experience of this performance—this book "concert"—you can always drop me a line at my email: kim@jeeyoonkim.com.

I cherish the moment when a concert is over, because I finally get to have a real conversation with the audience at the reception. Even though the concert has been always a two-way channel experience for both of us, there is still something left in me wishing to talk to you more.

I hope to continue being a part of your journey and to have you remain part of my journey.

Let's keep in touch.

Love,

Jeeyoon Kim

ACKNOWLEDGMENTS

My high school piano teacher, KyungLae Suk, always told me to dream big. She assured me that my understanding of the world around me was much more mature than my age at that time, and I could use that intelligence to my advantage for anything I did in life. She always told me I was gifted in my perseverance. What she planted in me then was that I could make a difference in my life with my very own efforts. I know for sure that every step I've taken to move forward was another stepping-stone toward a better version of me. Thank you, Teacher Suk! I wouldn't be the same person without your trust in who I could become.

"You have everything you need to express this piece of music well." That's what my piano teacher at Indiana University, Reiko Neriki, told me when I said I needed better "technique" to play a particular piece of music. She was puzzled by my comment and said it was not about the technique, but about the message in the music. I vividly remember that, at that moment, I walked out of another layer of my old obsessive shell as a pianist. Before then, in Korea, I'd been immersed in a competitive environment that asked for performances that were "cleaner" and free of errors. However, since that day in Indiana, I have stopped worrying about technique, knowing that I already had what I needed.

More importantly, I started to listen, really listen for myself, to every note, to the composers, to the listeners, and to the world around me, in order to connect and to express the message in the music. Mrs. Neriki taught me how to listen.

Mrs. Thickstun's bag always had some interesting goodies to aid in teaching piano, things she'd collected over the years as a piano teacher. In her piano classes for five-year-olds, she had an amazing way to connect with children, talking to them at their level, almost as if they were adults yet allowing them to think for themselves. I was always mesmerized to observe how she taught, envying those children who had started piano lessons with her, using those quality methods. She had the magical ability to make every concept more relatable, applicable, and practical. I was lucky to have met her when I did. After my eight years of higher education, she taught me how to use everything I've learned as a pianist and apply it to my albums, teaching, performance onstage and offstage, all from her educator's lens. Thank you, Mrs. Thickstun, for your kindness and wisdom.

"Only the impossible is worthy of your mind and time." That was what my dearest friend and author, Allen T. Brown, has always told me whenever I've had challenges in my life. He said there are always solutions, and I simply have to find one of them. He would kick my butt if I was using my energy to stay frustrated or feel down because of life's obstacles. His way of approaching life with curiosity, boldness, and a sense of humor has given me tremendous fuel to move forward as a pianist and a person. I am extremely lucky to have this source of positivity in my life. I've never met anyone as generous and curious as he is. Thank you, Allen. You are my hero.

When I finally received delivery of my new album, *Over. Above. Beyond.*, I jumped for joy. After all of my hard work, it was finally here in my hands. I immediately called to meet up with my friends Clara and Gary. I couldn't wait to share this joy with them. I feel lucky to have these incredible friends who truly want the best for me, who rejoice in my accomplishments, and who are there for me when I am in need. I truly rest my soul with them. I am blessed to have this spring of love in my life, and we get to share our life together. Thank you, my Musketeers.

At Beaver Island in Michigan, in the summer of 2019, my mother finally got to attend my solo concert in America. She hadn't heard me perform in sixteen years, as the circumstances hadn't been right for her to visit the United States, given that it required a lot of traveling and she didn't speak English and would need quite a bit of assistance. It was the first time since I'd become a professional concert pianist that Mom could be in the audience. When I walked out for my encore at the end of that concert, I acknowledged her being there in the audience for the first time and dedicated the final piece to her. I could sense her crying quietly. I held back my tears also. I closed my eyes, trying not to think of all the obstacles we've been through together, including a flashback memory of Mom supporting my music by herself at difficult times.

Since I came to America in 2003, we only see each other about once a year. But we are like one entity. She is always sending an internal signal to my soul, letting me know that I am protected, cared about, and incredibly loved. I've never met anyone as open-minded and intuitive as my mom is. She has given me a tremendous sense of freedom all through my life, guiding me to walk independently and resiliently. I am the luckiest person in the world to have been born as her daughter.

Also special thanks to Larry, who has been the best stepdad in the world for me and a wonderful husband for my mom. I love you both— to the moon and back.

Finally, and most importantly, I give thanks to God for everything I do and rejoice in him, the lover of my soul.

ABOUT THE AUTHOR

*A*ward-winning classical pianist Jeeyoon Kim delights audiences with a sparkling combination of sensitive artistry, broad emotional range, impeccable technique, and innovative concert experiences. A native of South Korea, Jeeyoon has inspired a dedicated and passionate fan base from around the world. As a performer, she defies convention by expanding on the traditional classical concert experience. Her 2016 debut album, *10 More Minutes*, features a conversation with the audience from onstage. For her next act, Jeeyoon collaborated with New York–based visual artist Moonsub Shin to create a multimedia masterpiece, *Over. Above. Beyond.*

Jeeyoon began studying the piano when she was just four years old, and her love of music and the piano propelled her through her undergraduate studies in piano performance in Korea. After moving to the

United States, she graduated with distinction with a master's degree and a doctorate degree in piano performance, all on a full scholarship from Indiana University's renowned Jacobs School of Music.

In pursuit of an even deeper understanding of music and wishing to refine her ability to share it with others, she earned another master's degree in music education, piano pedagogy, with a full scholarship from Butler University, where she simultaneously served as a faculty member. As a testament to Jeeyoon's abilities as an educator, she was recognized with the Top Music Teacher Award from Steinway & Sons for three years in a row, from 2016 to 2018.

Today, between performances at venues like Carnegie Hall, the Chamber Music Society in San Francisco, and the Stradivari Society in Chicago, Jeeyoon remains focused on finding new ways to connect with audiences and bring a fresh perspective to the magic of classical piano music. In 2020, she launched a fast-growing podcast dedicated to helping people of all musical tastes and backgrounds discover the beauty of classical music. *Journey Through Classical Piano* delivers short episodes that feature concert-like musical experiences and in-depth explorations of classical compositions, hosted by Jeeyoon.

Jeeyoon is an art activist, educator, podcaster, YouTuber, and award-winning performer who strives to connect with new audiences and help them discover the magic of classical music. During her COVID-19 quarantine, she is creating *[si-úm]*, a project that blends classical piano with poetry and spoken word performances. She also walks daily, teaches, and performs via livestreaming from her home. For more information, please visit www.JeeyoonKim.com.

"A force of nature who lives for that special
connection with a live audience"

-GORDON BROWN, Classical Radio XLNC-FM

"I urge you to make Jeeyoon Kim's acquaintance.
She is very much her own artist, and possesses that most
important quality, the ability to make you want
to listen to her."

-DAVE SAEMANN, *Fanfare* magazine

"Exquisite, absolutely phenomenal!
She is a perfect window for music to speak for itself.
That is a rare gift to the world . . ."

-SUSAN KITTERMAN, former artistic director
of New World Youth Orchestras